# C Pearls

# C Pearls

**Yashavant P. Kanetkar**

# BPB PUBLICATIONS
B-14, CONNAUGHT PLACE, NEW DELHI-110001

*FIRST EDITION 1997*

*Distributors:*

**MICRO BOOK CENTRE**
2, City Centre, CG Road, **Ahmedabad-380009** Phone: 6421611

**COMPUTER BOOK CENTRE**
12, Shrungar Complex, M. G. Road,
**Bangalore-560001** Phone: 5587923, 5584641

**MICRO BOOKS**
Shanti Niketan Building, 8, Camac Street,
**Calcutta-700017** Phone: 2426518, 2426519

**BUSINESS PROMOTION BUREAU**
8/1, Ritchie Street, Mount Road,
**Chennai-600002** Phone: 834796, 8550491

**BPB BOOK CENTRE**
376, Old Lajpat Rai Market, **Delhi-110006** Phone: 2961747

**DECCAN AGENCIES**
4-3-329, Bank Street, **Hyderabad-500195** Phone: 512280, 593826

**MICRO MEDIA**
Shop No. 5, Mahendra Chambers, 150 D.N. Road, FORT,
**Mumbai-400001** Phone: 2078296, 2078297, 2002732

**INFO TECH**
G-2, Sidhartha Building, 96 Nehru Place,
**New Delhi-110019** Phone: 643825, 6415092, 6234208

**INFO TECH**
B-11, Vardhman Plaza, Sector-16, Electronics Nagar,
**Noida-201301** Phone: 8531346

**COMPUTER BOOK CENTRE**
SCF No.-65, Sector-6, **Panchkula-134109**,
Chandigarh Phone: 561613, 567538

**Limits of Liability and Disclaimer of Warranty**

The Author and Publishers of this book have tried their best to ensure that the programmes, procedures and functions contained in the book are correct. However, the author and the publishers make no warranty of any kind, expressed or implied, with regard to these programmes or the documentation contained in the book. The author and publishers shall not be liable in any event for any damages, incidental or consequential, in connection with, or arising out of the furnishing, performance or use of these programmes, procedures and functions. Product name mentioned are use for identifications purposes only and may be trademarks of their respective companies.

All trademarks referred to in the book are acknowledged as properties of their respective owners.

**ISBN 81-7029-859-8**

Published by Manish Jain for BPB Publications, B-14, Connaught Place, New Delhi-110001 and Printed by him at Akash Press, Delhi.

*Dedicated to*
*Prabhakar Kanetkar*

iii

# *Thanks!*

A fter taking the first hesitant steps in book-writing few years back it has now become a passion for me. But as any author would testify a programming book cannot be written in isolation and one has to seek help from so many quarters.

The most important contributors in this book project were Prafull Rathod and Shakil Ali. They hunted the programs that were lying nooks and crannies of 20 different computers in my office, got them together, suggested improvements and did most of the layout work. In short, they were indispensable.

The actual production of books is a task that makes even strong men quiver. I wonder how Manish Jain of BPB manages the whole work so effortlessly. Many thanks to him for always keeping me on my toes.

A very special thanks to Seema and Aditya for patiently bearing the burden that a book project puts on their share of my time.

Finally, I would like to thank all the participants who have attended the my C classes and seminars; you may not realise how much of C programming I have learnt from each one of you and your questions. A tip of the hat for all of you!

# *Contents*

# *Introduction*

It is six years since I moved from Mechanical Engineering into computers and started tinkering around with C. Like thousands others I too was fascinated by its simplicity and flexibility. Over the years I wrote lots of C programs. This book is a collection of some of them which I think are innovative. They were more or less written in the same order in which they appear in this book. You are of course free to take your pick and zoom into any one which interests you.

The programs in this book don't teach you C programming. There are plenty of good text books on C which I believe are already fortifying your shelves. If you are not comfortable with C programming I would suggest you to go through the introductory text on C before dipping your hands here.

While writing the programs I have resisted the temptation of writing text book like programs sandpapered with error checks. The idea all along has been to give you a wealth of new ideas and let you carry the wealth in the direction you choose. I would be glad if you could grab a few of the programming ideas presented in this book and siphon them into your programs.

# *1* *Interaction with Mouse*

Graphical User Interfaces (GUIs) and mouse go hand in hand. Though some GUIs do exist which manage the show without a mouse, the mouse has more or less become a standard input device with any GUI worth its name. A mouse is used to point at the icons which form the menu in a GUI - much like the way a child points to something he wants. These point-and-shoot menus of GUI bring along ease and convenience alongwith all the added agility of the real-life look alike of the mouse. As a result, more and more packages today are not only menu driven, but are also mouse driven.

The use of a mouse requires a program to sense its presence. Just attaching the mouse to the computer is not enough. What we also need to do is load a device driver program that understands the mouse. A device driver is a program which senses the signals coming from the port to which the mouse is attached. On sensing the signals, the driver translates these into the related action on the screen. This device driver is usually available in a program called MOUSE.COM or WITTYMS.COM, which work with different variety of mice.

The mouse has a separate cursor (often called a mouse 'pointer') which looks like an arrow and functions in the same way as the normal cursor. As we move the mouse, the mouse pointer moves correspondingly. It is just like using arrow keys. The only difference being, the speed at which the mouse cursor moves is much faster than that of an ordinary cursor. If desired, we can even change the speed of the mouse pointer, and even its shape.

Once the mouse driver is loaded, the various mouse functions can be accessed by issuing interrupt number 0x33. By setting up the AX register with different values (service numbers), various mouse related functions can be called, some of which are illustrated in the following program.

```
#include "dos.h"
#include "graphics.h"

union REGS i, o ;

main( )
{
    int gd = DETECT, gm, maxx, maxy, x, y, button ;

    initgraph ( &gd, &gm, "c:\\tc\\bgi" ) ;

    maxx = getmaxx( ) ;
    maxy = getmaxy( ) ;

    rectangle ( 0, 56, maxx, maxy ) ;
    setviewport ( 1, 57, maxx - 1, maxy - 1, 1 ) ;

    gotoxy ( 26, 1 ) ;
    printf ( "Mouse Demonstration Program" ) ;

    if ( initmouse( ) == -1 )
    {
        closegraph( ) ;
```

```
            restorecrtmode( ) ;
            printf ( "Mouse driver not loaded." ) ;
            exit( ) ;
      }

      restrictmouseptr ( 1, 57, maxx - 1, maxy - 1 ) ;
      showmouseptr( ) ;

      gotoxy ( 1, 2 ) ;
      printf ( "Left Button" ) ;

      gotoxy ( 15, 2 ) ;
      printf ( "Right Button" ) ;

      gotoxy ( 55, 3 ) ;
      printf ( "Press any key to exit...." ) ;

      while ( !kbhit( ) )
      {
            getmousepos ( &button, &x, &y ) ;

            gotoxy ( 5, 3 ) ;
            ( button & 1 ) == 1 ? printf ( "DOWN" ) : printf ( "UP  " ) ;

            gotoxy ( 20, 3 ) ;
            ( button & 2 ) == 2 ? printf ( "DOWN" ) : printf ( "UP  " ) :

            gotoxy ( 65, 2 ) ;
            printf ( "X = %03d y = %03d", x, y ) ;
      }
}

/* initialises mouse */
initmouse( )
{
      i.x.ax = 0 ;
      int86 ( 0x33, &i, &o ) ;
```

```
        return ( o.x.ax == 0 ? -1 : 0 ) ;
}

/* displays mouse pointer */
showmouseptr( )
{
    i.x.ax = 1 ;
    int86 ( 0x33, &i, &o ) ;
}

/* restricts mouse movement */
restrictmouseptr ( int x1, int y1, int x2, int y2 )
{
    i.x.ax = 7 ;
    i.x.cx = x1 ;
    i.x.dx = x2 ;
    int86 ( 0x33, &i, &o ) ;

    i.x.ax = 8 ;
    i.x.cx = y1 ;
    i.x.dx = y2 ;
    int86 ( 0x33, &i, &o ) ;
}

/* gets mouse coordinates and button status */
getmousepos ( int *button, int *x, int *y )
{
    i.x.ax = 3 ;
    int86 ( 0x33, &i, &o ) ;

    *button = o.x.bx ;
    *x = o.x.cx ;
    *y = o.x.dx ;
}
```

Mouse can be used in text mode as well as in graphics mode. Usually it is used in graphics mode. Hence we must first change over to graphics mode. The function *initgraph( )* is responsible for switching the mode from text to graphics. DETECT is a macro defined in GRAPHICS.H. It requests *initgraph( )* to automatically determine which graphics driver to load in order to switch to the graphics mode. The *initgraph( )* function takes three parameters, the graphics driver, in our case, DETECT, which enables *initgraph( )* to figure out the driver to be loaded (in our case the driver is VGAHI.BGI, since we are using a VGA); the graphics mode and the path to the driver file. Here we are assuming the driver files are in the directory *c:\tc\bgi*. Thus the path is "c:\\tc\\bgi".

Once we are into graphics mode we call the functions *getmaxx( )* and *getmaxy( )* to obtain the maximum x and y coordinates in the current graphics mode. Then we draw a rectangle using the function *rectangle( )* and set the viewport area which restricts any drawing activity within the viewport.

Next we call the function *initmouse( )* to initialise the mouse. It checks if the mouse driver has been loaded or not (by issuing interrupt 0x33, service number 0) and then reports the status to *main( )*. If mouse is not initialised successfully then the *closegraph( )* function unloads the graphics driver and the *restorecrtmode( )* takes the screen back to the mode that the monitor was working in prior to the calling of *initgraph( )*, which in our case is the text mode. If you have loaded the mouse driver successfully then in all probability the mouse would be successfully initialised.

Most softwares today provide windowing feature. Not just windows on the screen as boxes, but windows that restrict cursor movement. Like a screen within a screen. If we define the size of the window then we can make sure that the cursor moves within it only. This is what programs like Windows and even DBMSs like Foxpro and dBase IV give us. There is nothing too difficult about it. It's just a matter of putting the right values in the right registers. In our program this has been achieved by the function *restrictmouseptr( )*. Next,

another function called *showmouseptr()* is called. It actually displays
the mouse pointer on the screen.

Both the tasks of restricting the cursor movement and displaying the
mouse pointer are achieved by invoking appropriate services available under interrupt number 0x33. In fact once the mouse driver has
been loaded anything to be done with the mouse is always done by
some service or the other available under interrupt 0x33.

Then we enter a *while* loop where we check to see which button has
been pressed and accordingly display either 'UP' or 'DOWN'. Ad-
ditionally, the current coordinates of the mouse pointer are also
displayed. If a key is hit from the keyboard we exit the loop.

Details of some of the more commonly used services are given below:

| Interrupt | Service | Purpose |
|---|---|---|
| 0x33 | 0x00 | Reset mouse and get status<br>Call with: AX = 0x0000<br>Returns:<br>AX = 0xFFFF  If mouse support is available<br>AX = 0x0000  If mouse support is not available |
| 0x33 | 0x01 | Show mouse pointer<br>Call with: AX = 0x0001<br>Returns: Nothing |
| 0x33 | 0x02 | Hide mouse pointer<br>Call with: AX = 0x0002<br>Returns: Nothing |
| 0x33 | 0x03 | Get mouse position and button status<br>Call with: AX = 0x0003<br>Returns: BX = mouse button status<br>Bit  Significance<br>0    left button is down<br>1    right button is down<br>2    center button is down |

| Interrupt | Service | Purpose |
|-----------|---------|---------|
| 0x33 | 0x04 | CX = x coordinate<br>DX = y coordinate<br>Set mouse pointer position<br>Call with: AX = 0x0004<br>CX = x coordinate<br>DX = y coordinate<br>Returns: Nothing |
| 0x33 | 0x07 | Set horizontal limits for pointer<br>Call with: AX = 0007H<br>CX = minimum x coordinate<br>DX = maximum x coordinate<br>Returns: Nothing |
| 0x33 | 0x08 | Set vertical limits for pointer<br>Call with: AX = 0x0008<br>CX = minimum y coordinate<br>DX = maximum y coordinate |

Figure 1

# 2 *Drawing with Mouse*

ow that we know how to initialise mouse, display the mouse pointer, hide it if required, get the current position of the mouse cursor and status of the mouse buttons we can put all this to use to do something worthwhile. Drawing rectangles using mouse, for example. I have written this program for a VGA, mono monitor in 640 x 480 resolution graphics mode. But it works even on other monitors with lower resolutions without making any changes.

```
#include "graphics.h"
#include "dos.h"
#include "alloc.h"

union REGS i, o ;
int midx, midy ;
char far *p1, far *p2, far *p3, far *p4 ;

main( )
{
        int gd = DETECT, gm, button, x, y, sx, sy, tx, ty, x1, y1, x2, y2 ;
```

```
if ( initmouse( ) == -1 )
{
    printf ( "\nMouse not loaded..." ) ;
    exit( ) ;
}

initgraph ( &gd, &gm, "c:\\tc\\bgi" ) ;

gotoxy ( 1, 1 ) ;
printf ( "Draw box....." ) ;

gotoxy ( 60, 1 ) ;
printf ( "Right button to exit" ) ;

do
{
    showmouseptr( ) ;
    getmousepos ( &button, &tx, &ty ) ;

    if ( button & 1 == 1 )
    {
        hidemouseptr( ) ;

        sx = x = x1 = x2 = tx ;
        sy = y = y1 = y2 = ty ;

        setcolor ( WHITE ) ;
        save ( x1, y1, x2, y2 ) ;
        rectangle ( x1, y1, x2, y2 ) ;

        getmousepos ( &button, &tx, &ty ) ;

        while ( ( button & 1 ) == 1 )
        {
            if ( x != tx || y != ty )
            {
```

```
                    setcolor ( BLACK ) ;
                    rectangle ( x1, y1, x2, y2 ) ;
                    restore ( x1, y1 ) ;

                    x = tx ;
                    y = ty ;

                    if ( x < sx )
                    {
                        x1 = x ;
                        x2 = sx ;
                    }
                    else
                    {
                        x1 = sx ;
                        x2 = x ;
                    }

                    if ( y < sy )
                    {
                        y1 = y ;
                        y2 = sy ;
                    }
                    else
                    {
                        y1 = sy ;
                        y2 = y ;
                    }
                    setcolor ( WHITE ) ;
                    save ( x1, y1, x2, y2 ) ;
                    rectangle ( x1, y1, x2, y2 ) ;
                }

            getmousepos ( &button, &tx, &ty ) ;
        }

    restore ( x1, y1 ) ;
```

```
                showmouseptr( ) ;
        }
    } while ( ( button & 2 ) != 2 ) ;

    closegraph( ) ;
    restorecrtmode( ) ;
}

save ( int x1, int y1, int x2, int y2 )
{
    unsigned area1, area2, area3, area4 ;

    midx = x1 + ( x2 - x1 ) / 2 ;
    midy = y1 + ( y2 - y1 ) / 2 ;

    area1=imagesize ( x1, y1, midx, midy ) ;
    p1 = farmalloc ( area1 ) ;

    area2=imagesize ( midx + 1, y1, x2, midy ) ;
    p2 = farmalloc ( area2 ) ;

    area3 = imagesize ( x1, midy + 1, midx, y2 ) ;
    p3 = farmalloc ( area3 ) ;

    area4 = imagesize ( midx + 1, midy + 1, x2, y2 ) ;
    p4 = farmalloc ( area4 ) ;

    if ( p1 == NULL || p2 == NULL || p3 == NULL || p4 == NULL )
    {
        closegraph( ) ;
        printf ( "Memory allocation error!" ) ;
        exit( ) ;
    }

    getimage ( x1, y1, midx, midy, p1 ) ;
    getimage ( midx + 1, y1, x2, midy, p2 ) ;
    getimage ( x1, midy + 1, midx, y2, p3 ) ;
```

```
        getimage ( midx + 1, midy + 1, x2, y2, p4 ) ;
}

restore ( int x1, int y1 )
{
        putimage ( x1, y1, p1, OR_PUT ) ;
        putimage ( midx + 1, y1, p2, OR_PUT ) ;
        putimage ( x1, midy + 1, p3, OR_PUT ) ;
        putimage ( midx + 1, midy + 1, p4, OR_PUT ) ;

        farfree ( p1 ) ;
        farfree ( p2 ) ;
        farfree ( p3 ) ;
        farfree ( p4 ) ;
}

/* initialises mouse */
initmouse( )
{
        i.x.ax = 0 ;
        int86 ( 0x33, &i, &o ) ;

        return ( o.x.ax == 0 ? -1 : 0 ) ;
}

/* displays mouse pointer */
showmouseptr( )
{
        i.x.ax = 1 ;
        int86 ( 0x33, &i, &o ) ;
}

/* hides mouse pointer */
hidemouseptr( )
{
        i.x.ax = 2 ;
        int86 ( 0x33, &i, &o ) ;
```

```
}

/* gets mouse coordinates and button status */
getmousepos ( int *button, int *x, int *y )
{
        i.x.ax = 3 ;
        int86 ( 0x33, &i, &o ) ;

        *button = o.x.bx ;
        *x = o.x.cx ;
        *y = o.x.dx ;
}
```

To draw the rectangle we need corner coordinates of the rectangle. The coordinates of the first corner are to be selected by moving the mouse cursor to the desired location and pressing the left mouse button. The coordinates of the other corner of the rectangle are chosen by dragging the mouse to the desired location keeping the left mouse button depressed. As this is being done the control rotates in a **while** loop, performing the following operations in turn:

(a)    Draw the box
(b)    Collect the key hit by the user
(c)    Erase the box
(d)    Redraw the box at new coordinates

Each time the box is drawn, the function **rectangle( )** is called with the starting coordinates (**x1, y1**) and the current mouse cursor coordinates (**x2, y2**). Obviously, first time through the loop, only a dot would be drawn in place of a rectangle, since this time the starting and current coordinates of the rectangle would be same. As the user proceeds to hit move the mouse, the current coordinates (**x2, y2**) change, drawing a new rectangle in the process every time through the loop. This draw-erase-draw cycle is broken either when the user confirms the second corner by releasing the left mouse button, or he decides to abandon the drawing altogether by hitting the right mouse button. What if the box is to be superimposed on an existing drawing? Would it not erase the existing drawing? No. This aspect is taken care of by the functions **save( )** and **restore( )**. **save( )** stores the current screen contents where the rectangle is to be drawn. After the rectangle is drawn and the arrow keys are hit, the current cursor coordinates are updated, and the current box is erased. Now, **restore( )** goes to work and restores the original screen contents. This cycle goes on within the **while** loop. Finally, when the user confirms the second corner coordinate, the rectangle is made permanent.

# 3 *Building Mouse Cursors*

In text mode the mouse cursor appears as a block, whereas in graphics mode it appears as an arrow. If we wish, we can change the graphics cursor to any other shape the way Windows or Ventura or any other graphics software does. The mouse cursor in graphics mode occupies a 16 by 16 pixel matrix. By highlighting or dehighlighting some of the pixels in this matrix we can get a mouse cursor of the desired shape. For example, the following bit- pattern can be used to generate the cursor which looks like an hour-glass.

```
1 1 1 1 1 1 1 1 1 1 1 1 1 1 1 1      0 0 0 0 0 0 0 0 0 0 0 0 0 0 0 0
1 0 0 0 0 0 0 0 0 0 0 0 0 0 0 1      0 0 0 0 0 0 0 0 0 0 0 0 0 0 0 0
1 1 1 1 1 1 1 1 1 1 1 1 1 1 1 1      0 0 0 0 0 0 0 0 0 0 0 0 0 0 0 0
1 0 0 0 0 0 0 0 0 0 0 0 0 0 0 1      0 0 0 0 0 0 0 0 0 0 0 0 0 0 0 0
0 1 0 0 0 0 0 0 0 0 0 0 0 0 1 0      1 0 0 0 0 0 0 0 0 0 0 0 0 0 0 1
0 0 1 0 0 0 0 0 0 0 0 0 0 1 0 0      1 1 0 0 0 0 0 0 0 0 0 0 0 0 1 1
0 0 0 0 1 0 0 0 0 0 0 1 0 0 0 0      1 1 1 1 0 0 0 0 0 0 0 0 1 1 1 1
0 0 0 0 0 0 1 0 0 1 0 0 0 0 0 0      1 1 1 1 1 1 0 0 0 0 1 1 1 1 1 1
0 0 0 0 0 0 1 0 0 1 0 0 0 0 0 0      1 1 1 1 1 1 0 0 0 0 1 1 1 1 1 1
0 0 0 0 1 0 0 0 0 0 0 1 0 0 0 0      1 1 1 1 0 0 0 0 0 0 0 0 1 1 1 1
0 0 1 0 0 0 0 0 0 0 0 0 0 1 0 0      1 1 0 0 0 0 0 0 0 0 0 0 0 0 1 1
0 1 0 0 0 0 0 0 0 0 0 0 0 0 1 0      1 0 0 0 0 0 0 0 0 0 0 0 0 0 0 1
1 0 0 0 0 0 0 0 0 0 0 0 0 0 0 1      0 0 0 0 0 0 0 0 0 0 0 0 0 0 0 0
1 1 1 1 1 1 1 1 1 1 1 1 1 1 1 1      0 0 0 0 0 0 0 0 0 0 0 0 0 0 0 0
1 0 0 0 0 0 0 0 0 0 0 0 0 0 0 1      0 0 0 0 0 0 0 0 0 0 0 0 0 0 0 0
1 1 1 1 1 1 1 1 1 1 1 1 1 1 1 1      0 0 0 0 0 0 0 0 0 0 0 0 0 0 0 0
       Mouse pointer bitmap                    Screen Mask
```

The one's in the mouse pointer bitmap indicate that the pixel would be drawn whereas the zeros indicate that the pixel would stand erased. It is important to note that the mouse pointer bit pattern is 32 bytes long. However, while actually writing a program to change the pointer shape we need a 64 byte bit-map. This provision is made to ensure that when the cursor reaches a position on the screen where something is already written or drawn only that portion should get overwritten which is to be occupied by the mouse cursor. Of the 64 bytes the first 32 bytes contain a bit mask which is first ANDed with the screen image, and then the second 32 bytes bit mask is XORed with the screen image.

The following program changes the mouse cursor in graphics mode to resemble an hour glass.

```
# include "graphics.h"
# include "dos.h"

union REGS i, o ;
```

```c
struct SREGS s ;
int cursor[32] = {
                        /* Hour-glass screen mask */
                        0x0000, 0x0000, 0x0000, 0x0000,
                        0x8001, 0xc003, 0xf00f, 0xfc3f,
                        0xfc3f, 0xf00f, 0xc003, 0x8001,
                        0x0000, 0x0000, 0x0000, 0x0000,
                        /* The mouse pointer bitmap */
                        0xffff, 0x8001, 0xffff, 0x8001,
                        0x4002, 0x2004, 0x1008, 0x0240,
                        0x0240, 0x0810, 0x2004, 0x4002,
                        0x8001, 0xffff, 0x8001, 0xffff,
                } ;

main( )
{
    int gd = DETECT, gm ;

    initgraph ( &gd, &gm, "c:\\tc\\bgi" ) ;

    if ( initmouse( ) == -1 )
    {
        closegraph( ) ;
        printf ( "\n Mouse not installed!" ) ;
        exit( ) ;
    }

    gotoxy ( 10, 1 ) ;
    printf ( "Press any key to exit..." ) ;

    changecursor ( cursor ) ;
    showmouseptr( ) ;

    getch( ) ;
}

/* initialises mouse pointer */
```

```
initmouse( )
{
    i.x.ax = 0 ;
    int86 ( 0x33, &i, &o ) ;

    return ( o.x.ax == 0 ? -1 : 0 ) ;
}

/* displays mouse pointer */
showmouseptr( )
{
    i.x.ax = 1 ;
    int86 ( 0x33, &i, &o ) ;
}

/* changes mouse pointer shape */
changecursor ( int *shape )
{
    i.x.ax = 9 ;  /* service number */
    i.x.bx = 0 ;  /* actual cursor position from left */
    i.x.cx = 0 ;   /* actual cursor position from top */
    i.x.dx = ( unsigned ) shape;  /* offset address of pointer image */

    segread ( &s ) ;
    s.es = s.ds ;  /* segment address of pointer */
    int86x ( 0x33, &i, &i, &s ) ;
}
```

# 4 *More Mouse Cursors*

In the last chapter we saw how to change the default mouse cursor. Once we know this we can think of building different shapes of mouse cursors each to signify a different operation or mode. This is what is done by Ventura to show in which mode are we working currently. The following program shows how this can be managed.

```
#include "graphics.h"
#include "dos.h"
#include "alloc.h"

union REGS i, o ;
struct SREGS s ;
int c[ ][32] = {
                /* Cursor 1. Hand-screen mask + pointer bit map*/
                0xe1ff, 0xe1ff, 0xe1ff, 0xe1ff, 0xe1ff, 0x0000,
                0x0000, 0x0000, 0x0000, 0x0000, 0x0000, 0x0000,
                0x0000, 0x0000, 0x0000, 0x0000, 0x1e00, 0x1200,
                0x1200, 0x1200, 0x13ff, 0x1249, 0x1249, 0xf249,
                0x9001, 0x9001, 0x9001, 0x8001, 0x8001, 0x8001,
                0xffff, 0x0000,
```

```
                    /* Cursor 1. Arrow-screen mask + pointer bit map*/
                    0xffff, 0xffff, 0xe003, 0xf003, 0xf803, 0xfc03,
                    0xfe03, 0xfc03, 0xf803, 0xf043, 0xe0e3, 0xc1f3,
                    0x83fb, 0x07ff, 0x8fff, 0xdfff, 0x0000, 0x0000,
                    0x1ffc, 0x0804, 0x0404, 0x0204, 0x0104, 0x0204,
                    0x0444, 0x08a4, 0x1114, 0x220c, 0x4404, 0x8800,
                    0x5000, 0x2000,

                    /* Cursor 1. Hour glass mask + bit map*/
                    0x0C00, 0x0000, 0x0000, 0x0000, 0x8001, 0xc003,
                    0xf00f, 0xfc3f, 0xfc3f, 0xf00f, 0xc003, 0x8001,
                    0x0000, 0x0000, 0x0000, 0x0000, 0xffff, 0x8001,
                    0xffff, 0x8001, 0x4002, 0x2004, 0x1008, 0x0240,
                    0x0240, 0x0810, 0x2004, 0x4002, 0x8001, 0xffff,
                    0x8001, 0xffff,

                    /* Cursor 1. Para-screen mask + pointer bit map*/
                    0x0000, 0x0000, 0x0000, 0x0000, 0x0000, 0x0000,
                    0x0000, 0x0000, 0x0000, 0x0000, 0x0000, 0x0000,
                    0x0000, 0x0000, 0x0000, 0x0000, 0xffff, 0xffff,
                    0xffff, 0x0007, 0x0007, 0xeee7, 0x0007, 0x0007,
                    0xeee7, 0x0007, 0x0007, 0xeee7, 0x0007, 0x0007,
                    0xeee7, 0xeee7
            } ;

main( )
{
    int gd = DETECT, gm, button, x, y, area, i, choice ;
    char *p ;

    initgraph ( &gd, &gm, "c:\\tc\\bgi" ) ;

    if ( initmouse( ) == -1 )
    {
        closegraph( ) ;
        puts ( "Mouse not installed!" ) ;
```

```
        exit( );
}

for ( i = 0 ; i < 4 ; i++ )
{
    changecursor ( c[i] ) ;

    showmouseptr( ) ;
    getmousepos ( &button, &x, &y ) ;

    area = imagesize ( x - 15, y - 7, x + 32, y + 24 ) ;
    p = malloc ( area ) ;

    getimage ( x - 15, y - 7, x + 32, y + 24, p ) ;
    putimage ( i * 48 + 1, 1, p, COPY_PUT ) ;

    rectangle ( i * 48, 0, ( i + 1 ) * 48, 33 ) ;
}

gotoxy ( 10, 25 ) ;
printf ( "Press any key to exit..." ) ;

choice = 1 ;
disp ( choice, p ) ;
changecursor ( c[choice - 1] ) ;

while ( !kbhit( ) )
{
    getmousepos ( &button, &x, &y ) ;

    if ( ( ( button & 1 ) == 1 )
    {
        for ( i = 0 ; i < 4 ; i++ )
        {
            if ( choice - 1 == i )
                continue ;
```

```
                    if ( y > 0 && y < 33 )
                    {
                        if ( x > i * 48 && x < ( i + 1 ) * 48 )
                        {
                            hidemouseptr( ) ;

                            disp ( choice, p ) ;
                            choice = i + 1 ;

                            disp ( choice, p ) ;
                            changecursor ( c[choice - 1] ) ;

                            showmouseptr( ) ;
                        }
                    }
                }
            }

        getch( ) ;
    }

    disp ( int choice, char *p )
    {
        getimage ( ( choice - 1 ) * 48 + 1, 1, choice * 48, 32, p ) ;
        putimage ( ( choice - 1 ) * 48 + 1, 1, p, NOT_PUT ) ;
    }

    /* initialises mouse */
    initmouse( )
    {
        i.x.ax = 0 ;
        int86 ( 0x33, &i, &o ) ;

        return ( o.x.ax == 0 ? -1 : 0 ) ;
    }
```

```
/* displays mouse pointer */
showmouseptr( )
{
    i.x.ax = 1 ;
    int86 ( 0x33, &i, &o ) ;
}

/* hides mouse pointer */
hidemouseptr( )
{
    i.x.ax = 2 ;
    int86 ( 0x33, &i, &o ) ;
}

/* changes mouse pointer shape */
changecursor ( int *shape )
{
    i.x.ax = 9 ; /* service number */
    i.x.bx = 0 ; /* actual cursor position from left */
    i.x.cx = 0 ; /* actual cursor position from top */
    i.x.dx = ( unsigned ) shape; /* offset address of pointer image */

    segread ( &s ) ;
    s.es = s.ds ; /* segment address of pointer */
    int86x ( 0x33, &i, &i, &s ) ;
}

/* gets mouse coordinates and button status */
getmousepos ( int *button, int *x, int *y )
{
    i.x.ax = 3 ;
    int86 ( 0x33, &i, &o ) ;

    *button = o.x.bx ;
    *x = o.x.cx ;
    *y = o.x.dx ;
}
```

# 5 *Freehand Drawing Using Mouse*

I n the last few chapters we have seen how to develop functions to initialise mouse, display/hide mouse cursor, get the current mouse coordinates, check status of mouse buttons, change shape of mouse pointer, restrict mouse pointer movement etc. Let us now try to put all these functions together to develop something useful. Like say, freehand drawing... the way it is done in softwares like Paintbrush, CorelDraw etc. Here is the program...

```
#include "dos.h"
#include "graphics.h"

union REGS i, o ;

main( )
{
    int gd = DETECT, gm, maxx, maxy, x, y, button, prevx, prevy ;
```

```
initgraph ( &gd, &gm, "c:\\tc\\bgi" ) ;

maxx = getmaxx( ) ;
maxy = getmaxy( ) ;

rectangle ( 0, 0, maxx, maxy ) ;
setviewport ( 1, 1, maxx - 1, maxy - 1, 1 ) ;

if ( initmouse( ) == 0 )
{
    closegraph( ) ;
    restorecrtmode( ) ;
    printf ( "Mouse driver not loaded" ) ;
    exit( ) ;
}

restrictmouseptr ( 1, 1, maxx - 1, maxy - 1 ) ;
showmouseptr( ) ;

while ( !kbhit( ) )
{
    getmousepos ( &button, &x, &y ) ;

    if ( ( button & 1 ) == 1 )
    {
        hidemouseptr( ) ;

        prevx = x ;
        prevy = y ;

        while ( ( button & 1 ) == 1 )
        {
            line ( prevx, prevy, x, y ) ;
            prevx = x ;
            prevy = y ;

            getmousepos ( &button, &x, &y ) ;
```

```
                }

                showmouseptr( ) ;
            }
        }
    }

initmouse( )
{
    i.x.ax = 0 ;
    int86 ( 0x33, &i, &o ) ;

    return ( o.x.ax ) ;
}


showmouseptr( )
{
    i.x.ax = 1 ;
    int86 ( 0x33, &i, &o ) ;
}

hidemouseptr( )
{
    i.x.ax = 2 ;
    int86 ( 0x33, &i, &o ) ;
}

restrictmouseptr ( int x1, int y1, int x2, int y2 )
{
    i.x.ax = 7 ;
    i.x.cx = x1 ;
    i.x.dx = x2 ;
    int86 ( 0x33, &i, &o ) ;

    i.x.ax = 8 ;
    i.x.cx = y1 ; i.x.dx = y2 ;
    int86 ( 0x33, &i, &o ) ;
```

```
}

getmousepos ( int *button, int *x, int *y )
{
    i.x.ax = 3 ;
    int86 ( 0x33, &i, &o ) ;

    *button = o.x.bx ;
    *x = o.x.cx ;
    *y = o.x.dx ;
}
```

In *main()* the loop *while (!kbhit())* allows the drawing of as many freehand drawings as the user desires. The process stops when the user hits a key from the keyboard. The freehand drawing begins on hitting the left mouse button, and grows as the mouse is dragged with the left button depressed. On releasing the left button that particular freehand drawing is terminated. When the actual drawing is in progress the mouse pointer is hidden, and it reappears when the mouse button is released.

# 6 *Menus Using Mouse*

Quite often we navigate within menus of bestselling softwares using mouse without thinking for a moment how these menus are developed. The following program shows how such programs can be written. Care has been taken to ensure that the menu would work for all memory models and for different types of adapters like CGA, VGA, EGA etc.

```
#include "dos.h"
#include "graphics.h"
#include "alloc.h"

char *menu[ ] = { "Samosa    ", "Sambarwada", "Dahiwada ", "Exit" } ;
union REGS i, o ;

main( )
{
    int gd = DETECT, gm, choice = 1, bill = 0, width = 0, i, count ;
    char **buffer ;

    initgraph ( &gd, &gm, "c:\\tc\\bgi" ) ;
```

```c
    if ( initmouse( ) == -1 )
    {
        printf ( "\nUnable to initialise Mouse..." ) ;
        exit( ) ;
    }

    count = sizeof ( menu ) / sizeof ( char * ) ;

    settextstyle ( TRIPLEX_FONT, 0, 3 ) ;
    displaymenu ( menu, count, 100, 100 ) ;

    for ( i = 0 ; i < count ; i++ )
    {
        if ( textwidth ( menu[i] ) > width )
        width = textwidth ( menu[i] ) ;
    }

    buffer = malloc ( sizeof ( menu ) ) ;

    savemenu ( menu, buffer, width, count, 100, 100 ) ;

    while ( choice != 4 )
    {
        choice=getresponse(menu, buffer, width, count, 100, 100);

        gotoxy ( 50, 15 ) ;
        printf ( "You selected %s ", menu[choice - 1] ) ;
    }
}

displaymenu ( char **menu, int count, int x1, int y1 )
{
    int i, h ;

    h = textheight ( menu[0] ) ;
```

```
        for ( i = 0 ; i < count ; i++ )
             outtextxy ( x1, y1 + i * ( h + 5 ), menu[i] ) ;
}

savemenu ( char **menu, char **buffer, int width, int count, int x1,
             int y1 )
{
    int i, x2, yy1, yy2, area, h ;

    h = textheight ( menu[0] ) ;

    for ( i = 0 ; i < count ; i++ )
    {
         x2 = x1 + width ;
         yy1 = y1 + i * ( h + 5 ) ;
         yy2 = y1 + ( i + 1 ) * ( h + 5 ) ;

         area = imagesize ( x1, yy1, x2, yy2 ) ;
         buffer[i] = malloc ( area ) ;

         getimage ( x1, yy1, x2, yy2, buffer[i] ) ;
    }
}

getresponse ( char **menu, char **buffer, int width, int count, int x1, int
y1 )
{
    int choice = 1, prevchoice = 0, x, y, x2, y2, button ;
    int in, i, h ;

    h = textheight ( menu[0] ) ;
    y2 = y1 + count * ( h + 5 ) ;
    x2 = x1 + width ;

    rectangle ( x1 - 5, y1 - 5, x2 + 5, y2 + 5 ) ;

    while ( 1 )
```

```
{
    getmousepos ( &button, &x, &y ) ;

    if ( x >= x1 && x <= x2 && y >= y1 && y <= y2 )
    {
        in = 1 ;

        for ( i = 1 ; i <= count ; i++ )
        {
            if ( y <= y1 + i * ( h + 5 ) )
            {
                choice = i ;
                break ;
            }
        }

        if ( prevchoice != choice )
        {
            hidemouseptr( ) ;

            highlight ( buffer, choice, h, x1, y1 ) ;

            if ( prevchoice )
                dehighlight (buffer, prevchoice, h, x1, y1 ) ;

            prevchoice = choice ;

            showmouseptr( ) ;
        }
        if ( ( button & 1 ) == 1 )
        {
            while ( ( button & 1 ) == 1 )
                getmousepos ( &button, &x, &y ) ;

            if ( x >= x1 && x <= x2 && y >= y1 && y <= y2 )
                return ( choice ) ;
        }
```

```
                }
                else
                {
                    if ( in == 1 )
                    {
                        in = 0 ;
                        prevchoice = 0 ;

                        hidemouseptr( ) ;

                        dehighlight ( buffer, choice, h, x1, y1 ) ;

                        showmouseptr( ) ;
                    }
                }
            }
}

highlight ( char **buffer, int ch, int h, int x1, int y1 )
{
    putimage( x1, y1 + ( ch - 1 ) * ( h + 5 ), buffer[ch - 1], NOT_PUT ) ;
}

dehighlight ( char **buffer, int ch, int h, int x1, int y1 )
{
    putimage( x1, y1 + ( ch - 1 ) * ( h + 5 ), buffer[ch - 1], COPY_PUT ) ;
}
/* initialises mouse */
initmouse( )
{
    i.x.ax = 0 ;
    int86 ( 0x33, &i, &o ) ;

    return ( o.x.ax == 0 ? -1 : 0 ) ;
}

/* displays mouse pointer */
```

```
showmouseptr( )
{
    i.x.ax = 1 ;
    int86 ( 0x33, &i, &o ) ;
}

/* hides mouse pointer */
hidemouseptr( )
{
    i.x.ax = 2 ;
    int86 ( 0x33, &i, &o ) ;
}

/* gets mouse coordinates and button status */
getmousepos ( int *button, int *x, int *y )
{
    i.x.ax = 3 ;
    int86 ( 0x33, &i, &o ) ;

    *button = o.x.bx ;
    *x = o.x.cx ;
    *y = o.x.dx ;
}
```

Note that the menu items are stored in an array of pointers to strings
*menu[ ]*. Once the graphics system and the mouse has been initialised
the number of items in the menu are determined, text style is set and
the menu is displayed on the screen using the function *displaymenu( )*.
To highlight or dehighlight the menu items rather than building the
items from scratch their existing images are stored in a buffer. The
space for this buffer is allocated using *malloc( )* and the actual saving
of images is done through the function *savemenu( )*. The base addresses of these images are stored in an array of pointers, pointed to by
the variable *buffer*. The actual movement of mouse pointer, highlight-
ing/dehighlighting of menu items and selection of a menu item is
done through the *getresponse( )* function.

To begin with the *getresponse( )* function checks the position of the mouse pointer. If the mouse pointer is inside the area occupied by the menu then it checks on which menu item is it placed and highlights that item. If the user attempts to move the mouse pointer outside this menu item then it is dehighlighted. If an item is highlighted and the left mouse button is clicked then it is assumed that the menu item has been selected and an appropriate value is returned. Observe that to highlight an item the *putimage( )* function has been used in such a manner that the existing image of the item is just reversed.

# 7 *How The Format Command Really Works*

We so often use the FORMAT command of DOS without sparing a thought about how it really works, what happens internally when we format a disk etc. The primary function of the FORMAT command is to place identification marks on the disk for every sector. Each identification mark is a 4-byte entry, and a unique entry is placed for each sector on the disk. This entry consists of Cylinder number, Side number, Sector number and FORMAT value. This entry is often called CHRN entry, standing for Cylinder, Head, Record and Numeric value. The Numeric values used for sectors of different sizes are as follows:

| Sector size | Numeric value |
| --- | --- |
| 128 | 0 |
| 256 | 1 |
| 512 | 2 |
| 1024 | 3 |

Using the ROM-BIOS disk format services the FORMAT command places unique CHRN values on the disk for each sector. The ROM-BIOS service uses the index hole to determine where to place the CHRN values. Once the disk has been formatted, the ROM-BIOS Disk I/O services use these CHRN values to locate specific sectors. By this time the index hole has served its purpose.

If we are to write our own FORMAT command we will have to do so in following steps:

(a)   Format a track using the ROM-BIOS Disk Format service (interrupt 19, service 5). While using this interrupt a buffer containing a 4-byte CHRN entry for each sector on the track needs to be set up.

(b)   Verify whether the track has been successfully formatted or not. If the track has not been properly formatted then record this fact in an array. This array would be later on used to mark the sectors belonging to the track as 'Bad' while building the FAT.

(c)   Repeat steps (a) and (b) for every track to be created on the disk.

(d)   Build the system areas like Boot Sector, FAT and DIR on the disk with appropriate values.

(e)   Report the available bytes, and bytes in bad sector, if any.

While using ROM-BIOS Disk Format service the values that are to be set up in various CPU registers are as shown below:

Register     Contents

AH           Service number (5, for disk format service)
AL           Number of sectors per track

| CH | Track number |
|----|--------------|
| DH | Drive number |
| DL | Side number |
| ES | Segment address of CHRN buffer |
| BX | Offset address of CHRN buffer |

Assuming that a buffer has already been set up with appropriate values of CHRN through some other function, let us try to write the *formattrk( )* function.

```
formattrk ( int drv, int side, int trk, int sec_per_trk, char far *chrn )
{
    union REGS i, o ;
    struct SREGS s ;

    i.h.ah = 5 ;
    i.h.al = sec_per_trk ;
    i.h.ch = trk ;
    i.h.dh = side ;
    i.h.dl = drv ;

    s.es = FP_SEG ( chrn ) ; /* segment address */
    i.x.bx = FP_OFF ( chrn ) ; /* offset address */
    int86x ( 19, &i, &o, &s ) ;

    if ( o.x.cflag != 0 )
        return ( o.h.ah ) ;
    else
        return ( 0 ) ;
}
```

Since *chrn* has been declared as a *far* pointer, to obtain the segment and offset addresses the macros FP_SEG and FP_OFF have been used. We will have to call the *formattrk( )* function repeatedly for each individual track.

That finishes the easiest part of the FORMAT command. We still have to see how to build the CHRN buffer and the system areas like Boot sector, FAT and DIR.

# 8 *Writing Our Own Format Command*

In the previous chapter we saw the steps involved in writing a FORMAT program. We even saw how the *formattrk( )* function formats an individual track and sets up CHRN values in it for each sector. Let us now see how to call this function to format the entire disk. The program given below shows this.

```
#include "dos.h"
#include "bios.h"
#include "alloc.h"
#include "stdlib.h"

char *fat ;
struct format
{
      unsigned last_side, trk_per_side, sec_per_trk ;
      unsigned sec_per_fat, sec_per_dir ;
} id[2] = {
```

```
                    1, 40, 9, 2, 7,
                    1, 80, 15, 7, 14
            } ;

main( )
{
    int i, dos_sec, drv = 0, side, trk, sec ;
    int status, bad_secs = 0, sm, fl ;
    char far *chrn ;

    clrscr( ) ;
    printf ( "\n1. 360 kb floppy 2. 1.2 mb floppy" ) ;
    printf ( "\nEnter your choice " ) ;
    scanf ( "%d", &fl ) ;

    fl -= 1 ;
    printf ( "Enter disk in drive A and press any key..." ) ;

    getch( ) ;

    if ( ( sm = setmedia ( fl ) ) != 0 )
    {
        if ( ( sm = setmedia ( fl ) ) != 0 )
        {
            printf ( "\nCan't format disk" ) ;
            exit ( 1 ) ;
        }
    }

    chrn = ( char * ) malloc ( 4 * id[fl].sec_per_trk ) ;
    fat = calloc ( id[fl].sec_per_fat * 512, 1 ) ;
    dos_sec = bad_secs = 0 ;

    for ( trk = 0 ; trk < id[fl].trk_per_side ; trk++ )
    {
        for ( side = 0 ; side <= id[fl].last_side ; side++ )
        {
```

```
                    gotoxy ( 10, 10 ) ;
                    printf ( "Head %2d Cylinder %2d", side, trk ) ;

                    setchrn ( chrn, id[fl].sec_per_trk, side, trk ) ;
                    formattrk ( drv, side, trk, id[fl].sec_per_trk, chrn ) ;
                    status = biosdisk ( 4, drv, side, trk, 1, id[fl].sec_per_trk, "" ) ;

                    if ( status != 0 )
                    {
                            sm = setmedia ( fl ) ;

                            if ( trk == 0 )
                            {
                                    puts ( "\nError: Track 0 BAD" ) ;
                                    exit ( 1 ) ;
                            }
                            else
                            {
                                    for ( i = 1 ; i <= id[fl].sec_per_trk ; i++, dos_sec++ )
                                    {
                                            markbad ( dos_sec, fl ) ;
                                            bad_secs += 2 ;
                                    }

                                    gotoxy ( 10, 10 ) ;
                                    printf ( "Error" ) ;
                            }
                    }
                    else  /* success */
                            dos_sec += ( id[fl].sec_per_trk ) ;
            }
    }

    writesys ( fl ) ;  /* build system areas */
    printstatistics ( fl, bad_secs ) ;
}
```

To begin with we have declared an array of structures *id[ ]* which is set up with specific values for 360 kb and 1.2 mb disks. Depending upon which type of floppy the user wants to format, that particular set of values from the array *id[ ]* are used for formatting the disk. Once the user has inserted the disk to be formatted in drive A we call a function *setmedia( )*. This function calls a ROM- BIOS service which sets up a 11 byte table in memory called 'disk base table' with information like head unload delay time, head load delay time, head settle time, disk motor startup time etc. This information is required by the ROM-BIOS disk format service. Next, through a pair of *for* loops we call the *formattrk( )* function for formatting individual tracks on each side of the disk. Before we call this function we set up the CHRN buffer by calling the function *setchrn( )*. Once a track is formatted, a call to *biosdisk( )* is made to check whether the formatting is successful or not. If unsuccessful, then the function *markbad( )* is called to mark the sectors in that track as 'bad'.

Once outside the loops the system areas like boot sector, FAT and DIR are built by the function *writesys( )* and the values of available and bad sectors is displayed by the function *printstatistics( )*.

That finishes one part of the program.

Let us now see how these functions are developed. They are given below with appropriate comments.

```
/* set up disk base table with relevant values */
setmedia ( int fl )
{
     union REGS i, o ;

     i.h.ah = 23 ;  /* service number */
     i.h.al = fl + 2 ;  /* floppy disk type code */
     i.h.dl = 0 ;  /* drive A */
     int86 ( 19, &i, &o ) ;

     return ( o.x.cflag ) ;
```

```
}

/* sets up a buffer with CHRN values for sectors on a track */
setchrn ( char far *chrn, int spt, int side, int trk )
{
    int sec , a ;

    for ( sec = 1 ; sec <= spt ; sec++ )
    {
        a = ( sec - 1 ) * 4 ;
        chrn[a] = trk ;
        chrn[a + 1] = side ;
        chrn[a + 2] = sec ;
        chrn[a + 3] = 2 ;
    }
}

/* mark sectors in the track which could not be formatted successfully
   as 'bad' */
markbad ( int dos_sec, int fl )
{
    int clno, off ;

    clno = 2 + ( dos_sec - ( id[fl].sec_per_fat * 2 +
                   id[fl].sec_per_dir ) ) / 2 ;
    off = clno * 3 / 2 ;

    /* write 0xFF7 in FAT to mark a bad cluster */
    if ( clno % 2 == 0 )
    {
        fat[off] = 0xF7 ;
        fat[off + 1] |= 0x0F ;
    }
    else
    {
        fat[off] |= 0x70 ;
        fat[off + 1] = 0xFF ;
```

```
        }
    }

/* writes FAT and DIR sectors on the disk */
writesys ( int fl )
{
    int s1, s2, i, j ;
    static char dir[512] ;

    /* mark media descriptor byte in fat */
    fat[0] = ( fl == 0 ? 0xFD : 0xF9 ) ;
    fat[1] = 0xFF ;
    fat[2] = 0xFF ;

    /* write two copies of FAT */
    s1 = abswrite ( 0, id[fl].sec_per_fat, 1, fat ) ;
    s2 = abswrite ( 0, id[fl].sec_per_fat, id[fl].sec_per_fat+1, fat ) ;

    /* if writing of FAT fails */
    if ( s1 || s2 )
    {
        printf ( "Error in writing FAT" ) ;
        exit ( 3 ) ;
    }

    /* initialize directory sectors with zeros */
    for ( i = 1 ; i <= id[fl].sec_per_dir ; i++ )
        abswrite ( 0, 1, id[fl].sec_per_fat * 2 + i, dir ) ;
}

/* calculates & prints the bytes available & bytes in bad sectors*/
printstatistics ( int fl , int bad_secs )
{
    long int tot, sys ;

    tot = ( id[fl].last_side + 1L ) * id[fl].trk_per_side *
    id[fl].sec_per_trk * 512L ;
```

```
        sys = ( 1 + id[fl].sec_per_fat * 2 + id[fl].sec_per_dir ) * 512L ;

        gotoxy ( 1, 17 ) ;
        printf ( "%8ld total bytes", tot ) ;
        printf ( "\n%8ld bytes in system area", sys ) ;
        printf ( "\n%8ld bytes in bad sectors", bad_secs * 512L ) ;
        printf ( "\n%8ld bytes avlbl", tot-sys-( bad_secs * 512L) ) ;
}
```

# 9

# *Load Install-able Fonts*

S everal Word-processors and DTP softwares provide numerous fonts to work with. Though a lot has been said about font generation in graphics mode not much literature is available about font generation in text mode. For example, what do I do if I am to generate Devanagari characters in text mode? For this Character Generation functions are available for MCGA, EGA and VGA+ adapters. These functions are grouped under interrupt 16, function 17. Function 17 provides a number of subfunctions to set and get character generation features on the MCGA, EGA, and VGA+ adapters. Obviously, different adapters have slight differences in implementation of these subfunctions. Following is the list of these functions.

| AL = | Character Generator Subfunctions | Adapters/Drivers |
|------|-----------------------------------|------------------|
| 0    | Load User Font                    | VGA+,EGA,MCGA    |
| 1    | Load 8x14 Font                    | VGA+,EGA,MCGA    |
| 2    | Load 8x8 Font                     | VGA+,EGA,MCGA    |
| 3    | Select Font Mode                  | VGA+,EGA,MCGA    |
| 4    | Load 8x16 Mode                    | VGA+,MCG         |
| 10h  | Load User Font After Mode Set     | VGA+,EGA,MCGA    |
| 11h  | Load 8x14 Font After Mode Set     | VGA+,EGA,MCGA    |
| 12h  | Load 8x8 Font After Mode Set      | VGA+,EGA,MCGA    |
| 14h  | Load 8x16 Font After Mode Set     | VGA+,MCGA        |
| 20h  | Set Int 1Fh Graphics Font Ptr.    | VGA+,EGA,MCGA    |
| 21h  | Set Int 43h Graphics Font Ptr.    | VGA+,EGA,MCGA    |
| 22h  | Load 8x14 Font into Int 43h       | VGA+,EGA,MCGA    |
| 23h  | Load 8x8 Font into Int 43         | VGA+,EGA,MCGA    |
| 24h  | Load 8x16 Font into Int 43h       | VGA+,MCGA        |
| 30h  | Get Font Information               | VGA+,EGA,MCGA    |

Figure 2

Although the list of subfunctions skips over some subfunction numbers, these are unused and will simply return without any action on an EGA/VGA adapter. Future adapters may assign currently unused subfunctions to new uses.

Let us now see how the ASCII character codes are converted into actual character shapes on the screen. For converting an ASCII character code into an array of pixels on the screen, a translation table or Character Generator is used. On older display adapters such as MA and CGA, the character generator was located in ROM. Newer adapters like EGA and VGA do not use a character generator in ROM. Instead, in these adapters character generator data is loaded into plane 2 of the display RAM. This feature makes it easy for custom character sets to be loaded. Multiple character sets (up to 4) may reside in RAM simultaneously. Each character set can have 256 characters.

Character width is fixed at eight pixels (this is stretched to nine for monochrome text). Character height is selectable from 1 to 32 pixels. The standard character sets which are provided with the EGA are the CGA character set (8 pixels wide by 8 pixels tall), and the enhanced colour character set (8 pixels wide by 14 pixels tall.) One of these character sets is automatically loaded by the BIOS when a text operating mode is selected. If a monochrome text mode is selected, the 8 x 14 enhanced colour character set is used, but several characters in the set are replaced with characters that are optimized for the 9 pixel wide monochrome character cell. Because of its higher resolution capabilities, the VGA also includes a 9 pixel wide by 16 pixel tall character set. Custom character sets can be loaded using the BIOS video services.

Irrespective of the character height being used, characters always begin on 32 byte boundaries. For instance, the 8 pixel by 14 pixel character set requires 14 bytes per character, so 18 bytes per character go unused in the character map.

The location of character maps in memory is shown below.

| Character Map A | Character Map B |
|---|---|
| 0000h to 001Fh   - Char.0 | 2000 to 201Fh    - Char.0 |
| 0020h to 003Fh - Char. 1 | 2020h to 203Fh  - Char.1 |
| 0041h to 005Fh - Char. 2 | 2040h to 205Fh   - Char.2 |
| .. | .. |
| .. | .. |
| 1FE0h to 1FFFh  -Char.255 | 3FE0h to  3FFFh - Char.255 |
| **Character Map C** | **Character Map D** |
| 4000h to 401Fh - Char.0 | 6000h to 601Fh - Char.0 |
| .. | .. |
| .. | .. |
| 5FE0h to 5FFFh - Char.255 | 7FE0h to 7FFFh - Char.255 |

**For VGA only:**

| Character Map E | Character Map F |
|---|---|
| 8000h to 801Fh - Char.0 | A000h to A01Fh - Char.0 |
| .. | .. |
| .. | .. |
| 9FE0h to 9FFFH - Char.255 | BFE0h to BFFFh - Char.255 |
| **Character Map G** | **Character Map H** |
| C000h to C01Fh - Char.0 | E000h to E01Fh - Char.0 |
| .. | .. |
| .. | .. |
| DFE0h to DFFFh - Char.255 | FFE0h to FFFFh - Char.255 |

Figure 3

Let us now see how this knowledge can be put to use to generate characters in Devanagari.

Internal to the adapter are a number of 32x256 font pages. Each 32-byte font block in a font page describes the bits to use for each text character. In most cases only a portion of the 32 bytes make up the complete character. For example, the EGA's standard 8x14 font is made up of 14 bytes. The character "T" appears as:

| Byte | Bits | | | | | | | |
|------|---|---|---|---|---|---|---|---|
|      | 7 | 6 | 5 | 4 | 3 | 2 | 1 | 0 |
| 0    | 0 | 0 | 0 | 0 | 0 | 0 | 0 | 0 |
| 1    | 0 | 1 | 1 | 1 | 1 | 1 | 1 | 0 |
| 2    | 0 | 1 | 1 | 1 | 1 | 1 | 1 | 0 |
| 3    | 0 | 1 | 0 | 1 | 1 | 0 | 1 | 0 |
| 4    | 0 | 0 | 0 | 1 | 1 | 0 | 0 | 0 |
| 5    | 0 | 0 | 0 | 1 | 1 | 0 | 0 | 0 |
| 6    | 0 | 0 | 0 | 1 | 1 | 0 | 0 | 0 |
| 7    | 0 | 0 | 0 | 1 | 1 | 0 | 0 | 0 |
| 8    | 0 | 0 | 0 | 1 | 1 | 0 | 0 | 0 |
| 9    | 0 | 0 | 0 | 1 | 1 | 0 | 0 | 0 |
| 10   | 0 | 0 | 1 | 1 | 1 | 1 | 0 | 0 |
| 11   | 0 | 0 | 0 | 0 | 0 | 0 | 0 | 0 |
| 12   | 0 | 0 | 0 | 0 | 0 | 0 | 0 | 0 |
| 13   | 0 | 0 | 0 | 0 | 0 | 0 | 0 | 0 |

Figure 4

While loading a user font, we need to supply only the number of bytes per character that make up the character cell. For an 8x14 font, the user font table will have 14x256 bytes. All font characters for text modes are stored in the red plane, plane number 2, in the high-resolution graphics memory area.

The following program puts this theory into a program to generate
the characters अ , ब , क , and ड when you hit A, B, C, D from
the keyboard.

```
#pragma inline

#include "dos.h"

main( )
{
    unsigned seg, off ;
    unsigned char far ( tbl[56] ) =
    {
        /* bitmap for अ */
        0x00, 0x00, 0xFF, 0x92, 0x0A, 0x0A, 0x12,
        0x7E, 0x12, 0x0A, 0x0A, 0x92, 0x62, 0x00,

        /* bitmap for ब */
        0x00, 0x00, 0xFF, 0x02, 0x3A, 0x66, 0x92,
        0x8A, 0x46, 0x3A, 0x02, 0x02, 0x02, 0x00,

        /* bitmap for क */
        0x00, 0x00, 0xFF, 0x08, 0x28, 0x5A, 0x89,
        0x99, 0x69, 0x0D, 0x0A, 0x08, 0x08, 0x00,

        /* bitmap for ड */
        0x00, 0x00, 0xFF, 0x04, 0x3C, 0x44, 0x40,
        0x3C, 0x02, 0x42, 0x22, 0x1C, 0x00, 0x00,
    } ;

    seg = FP_SEG ( tbl ) ;
    off = FP_OFF ( tbl ) ;

    _AH = 0x11 ;  /* service number */
    _AL = 0 ;  /* subfunction number */
    _BH = 14 ;  /* bytes per character */
    _BL = 0 ;  /* character set number */
```

```
    _CX = 4 ;  /* number of characters defined by table */
    _DX = 'A' ;  /* first character in the table */
    _ES = seg ;  /* store segment:offset of font table in ES:BP */

    asm push bp
    asm mov bp, off

    geninterrupt ( 0x10 );

    _DX = 'a' ;
    geninterrupt ( 0x10 );

    asm pop bp
}
```

To begin with we have stored the bitmaps of characters अ , ब ,क , and ड in the array *tbl[]*. Since each character is assumed to be of size 8x14 and there are four characters to be loaded the size of the array is kept as 56 bytes. To accommodate more characters you may add their bitmaps and increase the array size correspondingly. Next interrupt 0x10, function 0x10, subfunction 0x0 is called to load these bitmaps in character generator RAM. The same service is called once again to ensure that the Devanagari characters appear even for smallcase equivalents of A to D. Remember to compile the program using the TCC compiler by giving the command:

```
    C>TCC -Emasm.exe <filename>
```

# 10 *More About In-stallable Fonts*

The MA and CGA adapters permitted to use of only 1 character set of 256 characters generated by the ROM character generator. As against this, in EGA and VGA at a time two character sets may be active, giving them the capability to display up to 512 different characters on the screen simultaneously.

Suppose we are to write a program to demonstrate how two sets of characters can be used. Out of the two 256 character sets we can load only one set through our program, whereas the default character set can be used as the other set.

When two character sets are active the text attribute bit 3 selects which character set will be used when you type a key. Before we can use bit 3 for this purpose the normal foreground intensity function of text attribute bit 3 should be disabled. This is done by loading the second eight palette registers to equal the first eight palette registers. For this interrupt 0x10, function 0x10, subfunction 2 can be used.

Once this is done, we have to set the Character Generator Select Register to a value 4 to select characters sets 0 and 1. This enables the bit 3 in attribute byte to select either first or second set of 256 characters. This is achieved by calling interrupt 0x10, function 0x11, subfunction 3. Next we can use calls to *writestring()* function to show how the two different character sets can be used. Here is the program which implements all these details.

```
#pragma inline
#include "dos.h"

char far *scr = 0xB8000000 ;

main( )
{
    unsigned seg, off ;
    unsigned char far *equip = 0x410 ;
    unsigned char d_col[ ]={ 0,1,2,3,4,5,6,7, 0,1,2,3,4,5,6,7,0 } ;
    unsigned char far ( tbl[56] ) =
    {
        /* bitmap for अ */
        0x00, 0x00, 0xFF, 0x92, 0x0A, 0x0A, 0x12,
        0x7E, 0x12, 0x0A, 0x0A, 0x92, 0x62, 0x00,

        /* bitmap for आ */
        0x00, 0x00, 0xFF, 0x02, 0x3A, 0x66, 0x92,
        0x8A, 0x46, 0x3A, 0x02, 0x02, 0x02, 0x00,

        /* bitmap for फ */
        0x00, 0x00, 0xFF, 0x08, 0x28, 0x5A, 0x89,
        0x99, 0x69, 0x0D, 0x0A, 0x08, 0x08, 0x00,

        /* bitmap for ड */
        0x00, 0x00, 0xFF, 0x04, 0x3C, 0x44, 0x40,
        0x3C, 0x02, 0x42, 0x22, 0x1C, 0x00, 0x00,
    };

    clrscr( ) ;
```

```
seg = FP_SEG ( tbl ) ;
off = FP_OFF ( tbl ) ;

_AH = 0x11 ;  /* service number */
_AL = 0 ;  /* subfunction number */
_BH = 14 ;  /* bytes per character */
_BL = 1 ;  /* character set number */
_CX = 4 ;  /* number of characters defined by table */
_DX = 'A' ;  /* first character in the table */
_ES = seg ;  /* store segment:offset of font table in ES:BP */

asm push bp
asm mov bp, off

geninterrupt ( 0x10 ) ;
_DX = 'a' ;

geninterrupt ( 0x10 ) ;

asm pop bp

/* reload upper 8 palette registers */
_AH = 0x10 ;
_AL = 2 ;
/* load segment:offset of colour palette in ES:DX */
_ES = _DS ;
_DX = d_col ;

geninterrupt ( 0x10 ) ;

/* select active character sets */
_AH = 0x11 ;
_AL = 3 ;
_BL = 4 ;  /* block specifier (attb. bit 3=0 - set 0, attb. bit 3=1 - se

geninterrupt ( 0x10 ) ;
```

```
        writestring ( "ABCDEFG", 0, 0, 7 ) ;  /* use set 0 */
        writestring ( "ABCDEFG", 1, 0, 15 ) ;  /* use set 1 */
}

writechar ( char ch, int r, int c, int attb )
{
    * ( scr + r * 160 + c * 2 ) = ch ;
    * ( scr + r * 160 + c * 2 + 1 ) = attb ;
}

writestring ( char *str, int r, int c, int attb )
{
    while ( *str )
        writechar ( *str++, r, c++, attb ) ;
}
```

# 11
# *A Line Input Function*

Prompting the operator for a line of text, such as a name or number, is part of nearly every user interface, even the GUI-est. Often only a small area of the screen can be dedicated to this purpose, but the interface must occasionally accept more text than can fit into the area. Text that won't fit usually must be scrolled horizontally. The function called *line_input()* developed here performs this task just about anywhere on the screen. It requires only three interface functions:

(a)    *get_a_key()*, which sets up the two global variables *ascii* and *scan* with ascii code and scan code for each key that the operator strikes, without echoing it.

(b)    *gotorc()* which positions the cursor at a desired .location on the screen.

(c)    *writechar()* which writes a character and its attribute directly into VDU memory.

The *line_input()* function presented here is written for MS-DOS, but can be easily adapted to other environments by changing the interface functions and the codes used for control keys.

You can easily remove unneeded line editing features. The only control character that the function must recognize is the backspace ('\b'), which moves the cursor one place to the left.

The display area begins wherever the cursor is when *line_input()* is called, and it extends to the right the number of spaces specified by the *disp_len* parameter. The *txt* buffer supplies the text that is to be shown in the display area initially, and receives the edited input. The buffer must be large enough to hold the number of characters specified by the *txt_len* parameter, plus a terminating zero, and will ordinarily be larger than the width of the display area. The initial contents of the *txt* buffer are displayed left justified and the cursor is positioned at the beginning of the text.

Because operator input is an inherently slow operation, the function has been written to minimize the code size, not to maximize execution speed. It redisplays the entire display area after each keystroke. Consequently, its response can be quite slow if the display area is wide and output to the screen is slow.

The function displays a pair of arrows at each end of the display area to indicate when text has been scrolled off that end. However, this feature is easy to remove if it interferes with the rest of the display.

Of course, the display area and the arrows at each end must fit on the screen. At the right end, you usually need to leave one space between the arrows and the right edge of the screen so the cursor will not drop to the next line when the arrows are displayed.

The Home, End and Del keys and the left and right arrow keys are used for line editing. The Enter key is used to terminate the editing. It is easy, however, to add other terminator keys.

The *line_input()* function uses BIOS calls for keyboard input & positioning cursor and direct screen access for screen output. This makes the program run faster and it gives good results on the slowest PCs. However, it is not portable, except perhaps to another system that also features direct screen access.

Given below is the code for the program.

```c
#include "dos.h"

int ascii, scan ;
char far *scr ;

void main( )
{
    char txt[40] = "hello" ;
    int i ;

    scr = ( char far * ) ( ( biosequip( ) & 0x30 ) == 0x30 ?
            0xB0000000L : 0xB8000000L ) ;

    clrscr( ) ;

    gotorc ( 10, 2 ) ;
    printf ( "Address: " ) ;

    line_input ( txt, 10, 11, sizeof ( txt ) - 1, 20 ) ;
}

writechar ( char ch, int r, int c, int attr )
{
    char far *v ;

    v = scr + r * 160 + c * 2 ;
    *v = ch ; * ( v + 1 ) = attr ;
}
```

```
get_a_key( )
{
    union REGS i, o ;

    while ( !kbhit( ) ) ;

    i.h.ah = 0 ;
    int86 ( 22, &i, &o ) ;

    ascii = o.h.al ;
    scan = o.h.ah ;
}

gotorc ( int r, int c )
{
    union REGS i, o ;

    i.h.ah = 2 ;
    i.h.dh = r ;
    i.h.dl = c ;
    i.h.bh = 0 ;
    int86 ( 16, &i, &o ) ;
}

line_input ( char *txt, int r, int c, int txt_len, int disp_len )
{
    int pos = 0, hidden_characters_at_left, temp, i, l ;
    char *t ;
    char far *v ;

    for ( l = strlen ( txt ) ; l < disp_len ; l++ )
        txt[l] = '\0' ;

    for ( t = txt, i = 0 ; i < disp_len ; i++ )
    {
        if ( *t )
        {
```

```
            writechar ( *t, r, c + i, 112 ) ;
            t++ ;
        }
    else
            writechar ( ' ', r, c + i, 112 ) ;
}

while ( 1 )
{
    pos < disp_len ? gotorc ( r, c + pos ) : gotorc ( r, c + disp_len - 1

    get_a_key( ) ;

    if ( ascii == 0 )
    {
        switch ( scan )
        {
            case 71 : /* Home key */
                pos = 0 ;
                break ;

            case 79 : /* End key */
                pos = strlen ( txt ) ;
                break ;

            case 75 : /* left arrow key */
                if ( pos > 0 )
                    pos-- ;

                break ;

            case 77 : /* right arrow key */
                if ( pos < strlen ( txt ) )
                    pos++ ;

                break ;
```

```
                    case 83 :  /* Del key */
                         if ( txt[pos] != 0 )
                              strcpy ( txt + pos, txt + pos + 1 ) ;

                         break ;
               }
          }
     else
     {
     switch ( ascii )
          {
               case 13 :  /* Enter key */
                    return ;

               case 8 :  /* backspace key */
                    if ( pos == 0 )
                         break ;

                    pos-- ;
                    strcpy ( txt + pos, txt + pos + 1 ) ;

                    break ;
               /* insert new character to left of cursor */
               default :
                    if ( strlen ( txt ) < txt_len )
                    {
                         t = txt + pos ;
                         memmove ( t + 1, t, strlen ( t ) ) ;
                         *t = ascii ;
                         pos++ ;
                    }
          }
     }

     /* redisplay entire line */
     if ( pos > disp_len - 1 )
```

```
            hidden_characters_at_left = pos - ( disp_len - 1 ) ;
        else
            hidden_characters_at_left = 0 ;

        t = txt + hidden_characters_at_left ;

        /* display arrows at left end if necessary */
        v = scr + r * 160 + c * 2 ;

        if ( hidden_characters_at_left != 0 )
            * ( v - 2 ) = 174 ;
        else
            * ( v - 2 ) = '' ;

        /* display text and trailing spaces, if any */
        for ( i = 0 ; i < disp_len ; i++, t++, v+= 2 )
            *t ? ( *v = *t ) : ( *v = '' ) ;

        /* display arrows at right end if necessary */
        v = scr + r * 160 + ( c + disp_len ) * 2 ;

        if ( strlen ( txt ) > disp_len && *t != 0 && pos != txt_len )
            *v = 175 ;
        else
            *v = '' ;
    }
}
```

# 12 *Setjmp And Longjmp*

The C programming language does not let you nest functions. You cannot write a function definition inside another function definition, as in:

```
int fun1( )
{
      int fun2( )  /* such nesting of functions is not allowed */
      {
          .....
          .....
      }
}
```

Because of this restriction it is not possible to hide function names inside a hierarchy. As a result all the functions that you declare within a program are visible to each other. This of course is not a major drawback since one can limit visibility by grouping functions within separate C source files that belong to different logical units of the program.

C does, however, suffer in another way because of this design decision. It provides no easy way to transfer control out of a function except by returning to the expression that called the function. For the vast majority of function calls, that is a desirable limitation. You want the discipline of nested function calls and returns to help you understand flow of control through a program. Nevertheless, on some occasions that discipline is too restrictive. The program is sometimes easier to write, and to understand, if you can jump out of one or more function invocations at a single stroke. You want to bypass the normal function returns and transfer control to somewhere in an earlier function invocation.

For example, you may want to return to execute some code for error recovery no matter where an error is detected in your application. The *setjmp* and the *longjmp* functions provide the tools to accomplish this. The *setjmp* function saves the "state" or the "context" of the process and the *longjmp* uses the saved context to revert to a previous point in the program. What is the context of the process? In general, the context of a process refers to information that enables you to reconstruct exactly the way the process is at a particular point in its flow of execution. In C program the relevant information includes quantities such as values of SP, SS, FLAGS, CS, IP, BP, DI, ES, SI and DS registers.

To save this information Turbo C uses the following structure which is defined in the header file *setjmp.h*.

```
typedef struct
{
    unsigned j_sp ;
    unsigned j_ss ;
    unsigned j_flag ;
    unsigned j_cs ;
    unsigned j_ip ;
    unsigned j_bp ;
    unsigned j_di ;
    unsigned j_es ;
```

```
        unsigned j_si ;
        unsigned j_ds ;
    } jmp_buf[1] ;
```

This is a system-dependent data type because different systems might require different amounts of information to capture the context of a process. In Turbo C, *jmp_buf* is simply an array of ten 2-byte integers.

To understand the mechanics of *setjmp* and *longjmp*, look at the following code fragment.

```
    #include "setjmp.h"

    jmp_buf buf ;

    main( )
    {
        if ( setjmp ( buf ) == 0 )
            process( ) ;
        else
            handle_error( ) ; /* executed when longjmp is called */
    }


    process( )
    {
        int flag = 0 ;

        /* some processing is done here */
        /* if an error occurs during processing flag is set up */

        if ( flag )
            longjmp ( buf, 1 ) ;
    }
```

Upon entry to *setjmp* the stack contains the address of the buffer *buf* and the address of the *if* statement in the main function, to which *setjmp* will return. The *setjmp* function copies this return address as well as the current values of registers, SP, SS, FLAGS, BP, DI, ES, SI and DS, into the buffer *buf*. Then *setjmp* returns with a zero. In this case, the *if* statement is satisfied and the *process()* function is called.

If something goes wrong in *process()* (indicated by the *flag* variable), we call *longjmp* with two arguments: the first is the buffer that contains the context to which we will return. When the stack reverts back to this saved state, and the return statement in *longjmp* is executed, it will be as if we were returning from the call to *setjmp*, which originally saved the buffer *buf*. The second argument to *longjmp* specifies the return value to be used during this return. It should be other than zero so that in the *if* statement we can tell whether the return is induced by a *longjmp*.

The *setjmp/longjmp* combination enables you to jump unconditionally from one C function to another without using the conventional return statements. Essentially, *setjmp* marks the destination of the jump and *longjmp* is a non-local *goto* that executes the jump.

To reiterate what we have learnt, for local (within a function) transfer of control we can use the *goto* keyword. We now know how C implements nonlocal transfers of control by using the library functions *setjmp()* and *longjmp()*. Their prototypes are defined in a file called *setjmp.h*. It consists of:

- an array (of structures) called *jmp_buf*, which can be thought of as a label data-object-type.
- the function *longjmp*, which performs the nonlocal transfer of control.
- the macro *setjmp* which stores information on the current calling context in a variable of the type *jmp_buf* and which marks where you want control to pass on a corresponding *longjmp* call.

*longjmp* and *setjmp* are delicate functions. They violate the flow of control and the management of dynamic storage. However, they are still quite useful in a peculiar situation when we want to bypass the normal function call and return discipline.

The invocation of the *setjmp* macro usually appears in one of the following contexts:

(a)   The entire controlling expression of a selection or iteration statement

(b)   One operand of a relational or equality operator with the other operand an integral constant expression, with the resulting expression being the entire controlling expression of a selection or iteration statement

(c)   The operand of a unary ! operator with the resulting expression being the entire controlling expression of a selection or iteration statement.

(d)   The entire expression of an expression statement.

Thus we can write forms such as:

```
switch ( setjmp ( buffer ) )
if ( a < setjmp ( buffer ) )
if ( !setjmp ( buffer ) )
```

The typical layout of a situation in which one would think of using the *setjmp()* and *longjmp()* functions is shown below.

```
#include "setjmp.h"
#include "stdio.h"

jmp_buf buf ;

main( )
{
        /* some code goes in here */
```

```c
for ( ; ; )
{
        switch ( setjmp ( buf ) )
        {
                case 0 : /* first call to setjmp would return 0 */

                        process( ) ;
                        break ;

                case 1 :
                        printf ( "\nReporting Error" ) ;
                        break ; /* ensures that process( ) is restarted */

                case 2 :
                        printf ( "\nReporting Error" ) ;
                        return ; /* ensures that process is terminated */

                default :
                        printf ( "Reporting Error" ) ;
                        return ;
        }
    }
}

process( )
{
    int a, b ;

    /* some operations which result into a or b becoming null */
    if ( a == NULL )
        longjmp ( buf, 1 ) ;
    else
    {
        if ( b == NULL )
            longjmp ( buf, 2 ) ;
    }
}
```

The *setjmp* macro saves its calling environment in the variable *buf* for later use by the *longjmp()* function. If the return is from a direct invocation, the *setjmp* macro returns the value zero. If the return is from a call to the *longjmp()* function, the *setjmp* macro returns a non-zero value.

The *longjmp()* function restores the environment saved by the most recent invocation of the *setjmp* macro in the same invocation of the program, with the corresponding *jmp_buf* argument. If there has been no such invocation, or if the function containing the invocation of the *setjmp* macro has terminated execution in the interim, the behavior is undefined.

# 13 *Advanced Command Line Processing*

U nix command lines, with all their dots and dashes, sometimes approach Morse code in their unreadability. Nevertheless this concise method of specifying and passing parameters to programs has proved very user-friendly to frequent Unix users.

Unix carries out the command line processing using a standard library function called *getopt()* standing for get options from command line. However, under DOS, most often, command line processing is tackled using the usual *argc*, *argv* variables.

In this chapter, I am going to present the *getopt()* function. This function would provide a consistent and easily-programmed way to define the command-line structure. This function should be usable on any system, DOS or non-DOS, that supports C and the argc/argv program interface.

I have made the following assumptions while developing *getopt()*. (These assumptions are standard under Unix):

(a)     Any program that receives the command line arguments will adhere to the following basic format:

C> program_name [options] [other_arguments]

Here *program_name* of course is the name of the file being executed at the DOS prompt. You can omit both *options* and *other_arguments*.

(b)     An option is introduced by a hyphen ( - ) and can be one of two types:

(1)     A single-letter option, such as -g, -b, -c, etc.

(2)     An argument option, which is a single-letter option followed by exactly one mandatory argument. The argument may be flush up against the option letter or separated from it by white space (space and tabs).

(c)     *options* may be grouped after a single hyphen and their order is not important, so the argument list:

C> program_name -g -p -a -x -o filename

can be rewritten as,

C> program_name -gpa -x -o filename

or even

C> program_name -gpa -o filename -x

and so forth.

(d)   *other_arguments* are non-option arguments. They are not
      prefixed with a hyphen and not associated with an argument
      option. Examples of non-option arguments include filenames,
      such as the list of .OBJ object modules passed to the C
      compiler.

      They also include positional arguments, such as the source and
      target files in a copy command:

```
C> copy source target
```

The *getopt( )* function provides a simple mechanism for processing
command-line options. The inputs to *getopt( )* are the count of command line arguments *argc*, the array of arguments *argv*, and an
options string. The options string is composed of all the options
recognized by a program. A colon (:) following an option letter
indicates that in the command line there should be an argument
following the option. The grouping/ordering example given earlier,
*-gpa -o filename -x*, would be coded as *gpao:x*. Here the : after o
indicates that *-o* expects an argument whereas the others are single-
letter options.

Each call to *getopt( )* returns the next option letter from the command
line, the index of the current argument (in a global variable *optind*),
and, for argument options, the option's argument (in a global variable
*optarg*). In case of an invalid option given at the command line the
function returns a '?' as an option.

Allowing the user to mix options and arguments on the command line
adds to the user-friendliness of a program. In the simplest case, it lets
you easily recall a previous command and append a forgotten option.

Using *getopt( )* is fairly simple the first time and extremely simple
afterwards. Just cut and paste your original "template" and delete or
add the appropriate options. The following program shows the
*getopt( )* function as well as how to use it.

```
#include <stdio.h>
#include <string.h>

#define NONOPT ( -1 )

char *optarg = NULL ;
int optind = 1, offset = 0 ;

main ( int argc, char *argv[ ] )
{
    int choice ;

    clrscr( ) ;

    while ( ( ( choice = getopt ( argc, argv, "g:p:" ) ) != NONOPT )
              || optarg != NULL )
    {
        switch ( choice )
        {
            case 'g' :
                printf ( "\nyou entered g with argument %s", optarg ) ;
                break ;

            case 'p' :
                printf ( "\nyou entered p with argument %s", optarg ) ;
                break ;

            case NONOPT :
                printf ( "\n%s", optarg ) ;
                break ;

            case '?' :
                printf ( "\nWrong choice" ) ;
                break ;
        }
    }
}
```

```
int getopt ( int argc, char *argv[ ], char *optstring )
{
    char *group, option, *s ;
    int len ;

    option = NONOPT ;
    optarg = NULL ;

    while ( optind < argc )
    {
        group = argv[optind] ;

        if ( *group != '-' )
        {
            option = NONOPT ;
            optarg = group ;
            optind++ ;
            break ;
        }

        len = strlen (group) ;
        group = group + offset ;
        if ( *group == '-' )
        {
            group++ ;
            offset += 2 ;
        }
        else
            offset++ ;

        option = *group ;
        s = strchr ( optstring, option ) ;
        if ( s != NULL )
        {
```

```
                    s++ ;
                    if ( *s == ':' )
                    {
                        optarg = group + 1 ;
                        if ( *optarg == '\0' )
                            optarg = argv[++optind] ;

                        if ( *optarg == '-' )
                        {
                            fprintf ( stderr, "\n%s: illegal option -- %c",
                                        argv[0], option ) ;
                            option = '?' ;
                            break ;
                        }
                        else
                        {
                            optind++ ;
                            offset = 0 ;

                            break ;
                        }
                    }
                    if ( offset >= len )
                    {
                        optind++ ;
                        offset = 0 ;
                    }
                    break ;
                }
                else
                {
                    fprintf ( stderr, "\n%s: illegal option -- %c", argv[0],
                                    option ) ;
                    option = '?' ;
                    break ;
                }
            }
```

```
        return ( option ) ;
    }
```

I hope you would agree that the *getopt()* function developed here
provides a portable and well-defined command-line processing features. If you choose to use it, it offers a more user-oriented command
line syntax.

# 14 *Debugging Using Command Line Switch*

In C programs we frequently use command-line arguments to override default values, display help, and control special options. C tackles command line arguments using the usual *argc* and *argv* variables. Whatever their use, the program almost always knows what to expect. This rigidity is appropriate for the arguments that control the main features of a program since these features aren't likely to change during the program's life. However, if we are to use command-line arguments as an aid to debugging we need a more flexible method to deal with them.

In a big program to monitor how the control is flowing programmers often add a *printf( )* statement at a certain place in the code. Then the programmer makes a provision to ensure that this *printf( )* gets executed during test runs and is deactivated during normal execution.

This is achieved by combining a special switch variable, let's say *debug*, with a simple test as shown below:

```
if ( debug )
    printf ( "Control has reached beyond the while loop" ) ;
```

The program is then made to examine the command-line arguments for a flag. If the flag exists, the program sets debug to *TRUE*, and to FALSE otherwise. However, in a large program where you need to incorporate this feature (switches based on command-line arguments), an explicitly-coded test for each switch becomes quite cumbersome.In such cases we can think of using a pre-defined number of switches. For example, using bit operations we can pack several switches into one variable:

```
if ( debug & BIT_MASK_1 )
    printf ( "Control has reached beyond the while loop" ) ;
```

This approach conserves memory and simplifies the command-line processing since a single numeric parameter can represent many switch settings. However, we are still limited to use some pre-determined, finite number of switches. Moreover, the programmer needs to remember which bit in the variable stands for which switch.

A more preferable option would be to permit an unlimited number of switches from the command line. This can be achieved by using a pre-defined ANSI-C macro called __LINE__. Whenever we use this macro in our program the preprocessor replaces __LINE__ with the line number in which the macro is present. Thus, if we use this macro we can automatically identify the location of any statement in the source code. Instead of identifying line number of each statement in the program we should logically divide the entire source code into distinct parts and note down their starting and ending line numbers in the program file. Then whenever we want to check whether the control has gone to a particular area we can supply the line numbers at the command line as shown below:

```
C> myprog ~10,50 ~100,175 ~200
```

Each set of line numbers begins with a ~ to separate them out from
other command-line arguments. This command line indicates that we
wish to be informed if the control reaches the range specified by the
line numbers. The last argument indicates that if only the starting line
number is provided then the ending line number should be assumed
as some sufficiently big line number.

Thus, determining whether a switch is on is a matter of identifying
its location in the code and then determining if that location is within
the bounds of an "enabled" area. To implement this we just need to
develop two functions, one to examine the command line (*parse()*),
and another to check whether a switch has been set or not
(*is_switch_on()*). These functions are given below. Next time we
would see how these functions can be used effectively in our program.
Sounds complicated? Well, the following program would unentangle
it.

```c
#include "stdio.h"
#include "stdlib.h"

#define MAX 20

struct bounds
{
    int min ;
    int max ;
} ;
struct bounds area[MAX] ;

#define DEBUG( x ) if ( is_switch_on ( __LINE__ )) { x; getch( ) ; }

main ( int argc, char *argv[ ] )
{
    int ch, a, i, num, j, no ;
    long int p ;
```

```
parse ( argc, argv ) ;

while ( 1 )
{
    printf( "\n1. odd/even 2. Prime no. 3. Factorial 0. Exit" ) ;
    printf( "\nYour choice? " ) ;

    fflush ( stdin ) ;
    scanf ( "%d", &ch ) ;

    switch ( ch )
    {
        case 1 :
            DEBUG ( printf ( "\nControl has reached case 1...
                    Press any key" ) )

            printf ( "\nEnter any number: " ) ;

            fflush ( stdin ) ;
            scanf ( "%d", &a ) ;

            a % 2 == 0 ? printf ( "Even" ) : printf ( "Odd" ) ;
            break ;

        case 2:
            DEBUG ( printf ( "\nControl has reached case 2...
                    Press any key" ) )
            printf ( "\nEnter any number: " ) ;
            scanf ( "%d", &num ) ;

            for ( i = 2 ; i <= ( num - 1 ) ; i++ )
            {
                if ( num % i == 0)
                {
                    printf ( "Not a prime no." ) ;
                    break ;
```

```
                        }
                }
                if ( i == num )
                        printf( "Number is prime" ) ;

                break ;


        case 3 :
                DEBUG ( printf ( "\nControl has reached case 3...
                                Press any key" ) )

                printf ( "\nEnter any number: " ) ;
                scanf ( "%d", &no ) ;

                for ( j = 1, p = 1 ; j <= no ; j++ )
                        p = p * j ;

                printf( "%ld", p ) ;
                break ;

        case 0:
                DEBUG ( printf ( "\nProgram about to terminate...
                                Press any key" ) )
                exit ( 0 ) ;
        }

        printf ( "\nPress any key..." ) ;
        getch( ) ;
    }
}

parse ( int ac, char *av[ ] )
{
    int i, k = 0, j ;
    char str[10], *s ;

    for ( i = 1 ; i <= ac ; i++ )
```

```
        {
            if ( *av[i] == '~' )
            {
                s = ++av[i] ;
                if ( strchr ( s, ',' ) != NULL )
                {
                    for ( j = 0 ; *s != ',' ; j++ )
                    {
                        str[j] = *s ; s++ ;
                    }
                    str[j] = '\0' ;

                    area[k].min = atoi ( str ) ;
                    area[k].max = atoi ( ++s ) ;
                }
                else
                {
                    area[k].min = atoi ( s ) ;
                    area[k].max = 10000 ;
                }

                k++ ;
            }
        }
    }

    is_switch_on ( int lno )
    {
        int i ;

        for ( i = 0 ; i < MAX ; i++ )
        {
            if ( area[i].min <= lno && lno <= area[i].max )
                return ( 1 ) ;
        }
        return ( 0 ) ;
```

}

*parse()* is the first function to be called from *main()*. It uses the standard *argc, argv* mechanism to access the command-line arguments. It examines the command-line and sets up the starting and ending line numbers in the array of structures *area[]* to identify different areas in the program which you wish to monitor. Enabled areas are specified at command line by a string of comma-separated fields following the ~ character. For example, if we wish to monitor when the control reaches case 1 and case 3 in the program given above, our command line would look like this:

        C> myprog ~25,31 ~47,54

During preprocessing the DEBUG macro is expanded. This expansion results into a call to the function *is_switch_on()*. This macro allows each switch call to use the same arguments regardless of location:

        is_switch_on ( __LINE__ )

This function returns *1* only if the specified line number falls within any of the "enabled" program areas. This is determined by examining the array *area[]* which has earlier been set up by the function *parse()*.

The *is_switch_on()* function doesn't modify the arguments, and thus will not affect the behavior of other code that uses *argc* and *argv*. The macro hides the repetitive details of the switch function call.

With this method you'll never run out of switches. As long as the source code is available, you can readily identify which switch you need to set for a particular test. You can improve this program further by using the pre-defined macro *__FILE__* which identifies the file being executed.

# *15* *Allocating Multiple Char Arrays*

When we are to copy a record from a file into memory we may have to allocate memory using the standard library function *malloc()*. Several approaches can be used for this allocation. For the sake of simplicity we would assume that all fields in the record are strings whose maximum lengths are known in advance.

The simplest allocation can be coded as,

```
ptr = malloc ( recsize ) ;
```

where *ptr* represents a pointer declared in your code and *recsize* represents the total record size. The base address of the allocated chunk is returned by *malloc()* and collected in *ptr*.

However, this simple allocation may prove to be inadequate if we are to allocate space for an array of pointers to strings, where each element (pointer) of the array points to a string. This is because only *ptr* would be initialised to a certain address. None of the pointers in the array that *ptr* accesses are initialized.

To use the pointers *ptr[i]* to designate strings, we must assign each its own portion of memory as shown below.

```
for ( i = 0 ; i < limit ; i++)
    ptr[i] = malloc ( size[i] ) ;
```

The *for* loop calls *malloc()* for each pointer *ptr[i]*. Counting the original call, creating N fields would require N+1 calls to *malloc()*. The overhead of function calls and allocation bookkeeping now begins to mount.

Also we will have to call *free()* N+1 times to release the memory when it is no longer needed. Forgetting to free *ptr[i]*, and simply freeing the original pointer *ptr* releases only one of the N+1 allocations. The rest remain allocated, and their memory becomes inaccessible.

A better scheme would be to sum the field lengths, and call *malloc()* only twice: once to allocate space for the array of pointers, and once to allocate the space to which these pointers will point.

This approach still lacks finesse. If *ptr* points to a single database record, a single call to *free()* should release the memory. However, since *malloc()* was called twice to create the record, you must call *free()* twice in its disposal.

We can overcome these problems by calculating the total memory required for the array of pointers plus the fields that these pointers will reference. A single call to *malloc()* can then allocate the required memory in a single block. Our program should then divide this space between the pointers and the referenced fields. The field addresses should be assigned to the pointer array and initialise the string space. Later a single call to *free()* would free the entire allocated block.

The following program shows how this can be achieved...

```c
#include "mem.h"
#include "conio.h"
#include "alloc.h"

#define findsize( x ) ( sizeof ( x ) /sizeof ( x[1] ) )

/* a sample database field set: */
char *fields[ ] =    {
                                " FName", " LName", " Address",
                                " City", " State", " Pin", " Remarks",
                        } ;

/* field lengths for sample database */
int sz[ ] = { 20, 20, 40, 15, 15, 7, 50 } ;

main( )
{
    char **create_record ( int, int *, int ) ;
    char **set ;
    int fieldcount, i, r = 1 ;

    fieldcount = findsize ( sz ) ;
    set = create_record ( fieldcount, sz, '_') ;

    if ( !set )
    {
        printf ( "\nError allocating memory for record\n" ) ;
        exit ( 1 ) ;
    }

    clrscr( ) ;

    for ( i = 0 ; i < fieldcount ; i++, r++ )
    {
        printf ( "%s: ", fields[i] ) ;
```

```
            gotoxy ( 20, r ) ;
            printf ( "[%s]\n", set[i] ) ;
            getstring ( set[i], sz[i], 21, r ) ;
            printf ( "%s\n", set[i] ) ;
      }

      puts ( "\nPress key..." ) ;
      getch( ) ;

      free ( set ) ;
}

char **create_record ( int num, int *flen, int initchar )
{
      char **field ;  /* this value is returned */
      char *p ;
      int i, recsize = 0, memsize ;

      for ( i = 0 ; i < num ; i++ )
            recsize += flen[i] ;  /* sum field sizes */

      recsize += num ;  /* add space for a terminator for each field */

      /* total to allocate includes space for strings and pointers to them: */
      memsize = num * sizeof ( char * ) + recsize * sizeof ( char ) ;
      field = ( char ** ) malloc ( memsize ) ;

      if ( field == NULL )
      {
            #ifdef ERR_INTERNAL
                  puts ( "malloc failure in create_record( )" ) ;
                  exit ( 1 ) ;  /* abort on failure */
            #else
                  return ( NULL ) ;  /* return warning */
            #endif
      }
```

```
        /* initialize strings */
        memset ( field, initchar, memsize ) ;

        /* set p to point to the first byte beyond the last pointer needed: */
        p = ( char * ) ( field + num ) ;

        for ( i = 0 ; i < num ; i++ )
        {
            field[i] = p ;  /* initialize the pointer array */
            p = p + flen[i] - 1 ;  /* get address of last char of the field */
            *p = '\0' ;  /* terminate the string */
            p++ ;  /* next string start address */
        }

        return field ;
}

getstring ( char *s, int size, int c, int r )
{
        int i ;
        char ch ;

        gotoxy ( c, r ) ;

        for ( i = 0 ; i < size - 1 ; i++ )
        {
            ch = getche( ) ;

            if ( ch == '\r' )
                break ;

            *s = ch ;
        }

        *s = '\0' ;
}
```

The function *create_record()* implements the strategy discussed earlier. Following this the code of the function *getstring()* is given which receives the string from the keyboard and stores into the memory that has been allocated by *create_record()*.

The operation of the function *create_record()* is best explained in database terms: records, fields, and field lengths. *create_record()* takes three parameters: an integer *num* that gives the number of fields in a database record, a pointer (*int \*flen*) pointing to an integer array (*int sz[ ]*) of field lengths, and an initialization character *initchar*. the initialization character is typically '\0' or space or an underscore. *create_record()* performs a single memory allocation and returns one pointer to the allocated memory. The pointer points to an array of initialised pointers to *char*. These point in turn to a set of strings located in the allocated block following the pointer array. Each string is itself initialized to the *initchar* character value.

We can now safely conclude that out of the different allocation strategies that can be used to allocate memory for a record when it is to be read into memory from the disk or the keyboard the scheme which uses minimum calls to the functions *malloc()* and *free()* would be the best one to adopt since it keeps the overheads of function calls and the allocation book-keeping to a minimum.

# 16 *The touch Utility*

Most Unix systems provide a small but a very handy utility called *touch*. Most of the times this utility is used to set the date and time of one or more files to the current date and time, that is, the date and time shown by the system clock at the moment when this utility is run. It can also be used to create zero byte files with the current date and time. DOS systems do not come with this useful utility, although some compiler vendors do provide one. Here I would show how this utility can be developed under DOS. In addition to features mentioned above the program given below allows you to specify a date and time to use in place of the current system date/time.

```
#include "stdio.h"
#include "string.h"
#include "io.h"
#include "fcntl.h"
#include "sys/types.h"
#include "sys/stat.h"
#include "dos.h"
```

```
struct T
{
    unsigned int seconds :5 ;
    unsigned int minutes :6 ;
    unsigned int hours  :5 ;
} tm ;
struct D
{
    unsigned int day :5 ;
    unsigned int month :4 ;
    unsigned int year :7 ;
} dt ;
int pos = 1 ;

main ( int argc, char *argv[ ] )
{
    int touch_file ( char *, int, int ) ;
    int process_args ( char **argv ) :
    int a ;

    if ( argc < 2 )
        usage( ) ;

    process_args ( argv ) ;

    for ( ; pos < argc ; pos++)
    {
        a = touchfile ( argv[pos], tm, dt ) ;

        if ( a == -1 )
            printf ( "Cannot reset date/time of file %s\n", argv[pos] ) ;
    }
}

int touchfile ( char *filename, int tt, int dd )
{
    int handle ;
```

```
        union REGS i, o ;

        handle = open ( filename, O_RDWR I O_CREAT, S_IREAD I
                        S_IWRITE ) ;

        if ( handle < 0 )
            return ( -1 ) ;

        i.h.ah = 0x57 ;
        i.h.al = 1 ;
        i.x.bx = handle ;
        i.x.cx = tt ;
        i.x.dx = dd ;
        int86 ( 0x21, &i, &o ) ;

        close ( handle ) ;
        return ( 0 ) ;
}

usage( )
{
        printf ( "Usage: touch [-t date] <files>\n") ;
        printf ( "Examples:\n") ;
        printf ( "touch <files>\n") ;
        printf ( "touch -t yymmddhhmmss <files>\n") ;
        printf ( "The first form sets the timestamp of files to the  "
                 "then-current time.\n"
                 "The second form sets the timestamp of files "
                 "to the specified time.\n" ) ;

        exit ( 0 ) ;
}

int process_args( char *argv[ ] )
{
        char datetime[13], d[3], m[3], y[3], h[3], mm[3], s[3] ;
        struct date dosdt ;
```

```
struct time dostm ;

if ( strcmp ( argv[1], "-t" ) == 0 )
{
    strcpy ( datetime, argv [2]) ;

    sscanf ( datetime, "%2s%2s%2s%2s%2s%2s", d, m, y, h, mm, s ) ;

    dt.day = atoi ( d ) ;
    dt.month = atoi ( m ) ;
    dt.year = atoi ( y ) - 80 ;
    tm.hours = atoi ( h ) ;
    tm.minutes = atoi ( mm ) ;
    tm.seconds = atoi ( s ) / 2 ;

    pos += 2 ;
}
else
{
    getdate( &dosdt ) ;
    gettime( &dostm ) ;

    dt.day = dosdt.da_day ;
    dt.month = dosdt.da_mon ;
    dt.year = dosdt.da_year - 1980 ;
    tm.hours = dostm.ti_hour ;
    tm.minutes = dostm.ti_min ;
    tm.seconds = dostm.ti_sec ;
}
}
```

# *17* *A Generic*
## *Search Routine*

Imagine a database having employee records each record containing name, age and salary of an employee. If we are to query each field we may be required to write separate code to search each field in the master structure array. In this chapter, I'll show how to use void pointers and pointer arithmetic to implement a single search routine that will handle searching all fields regardless of their data type. By taking advantage of these tools, a programmer can save time, reduce code size and simplify program maintenance.

For the employee record the structure declaration would be as follows:

```
struct emp
{
    char name[20] ;
    int age ;
    float salary ;
};
```

Assume that the database program can perform a query on all of these fields. For example, one legal query could be

```
find a salary = 3500.75
```

You could satisfy this query by creating a search routine to loop through all employee records looking for a salary 3500.75. In the same vein, you could write a separate search routine to handle the other fields name and age. This approach would be reasonable if all structures were this small. However, imagine the amount of code necessary for a structure of 50 fields? Worse still is the fact that a code change is required every time a new field is added or an existing one is modified. How can this query, or any other query be satisfied with one search routine?

The query must be parsed and the information it contains extracted. How the parsing is done is not a major concern for this discussion. It is part of the user interface, not the database system. However, the information that the line contains is crucial. The search is interested in two pieces of information: the keyword *salary* and the value *3500.75*. First, you must determine if this information is valid. If *salary* is not a field in the master structure, there is nothing with which to compare it.

In short, you must define whether a keyword is valid, define its data type, and determine where it is located in the employee structure. All of the information needed to solve this problem can reside in a structure called *field* shown below:

```
struct field
{
    char keyword[20] ;
    int type ;
    struct emp *ptr ;
} ;
```

Here the field *keyword[]* defines a legal field name. By using the employee structure as a guide, the valid keywords acceptable to this application are *name*, *age* and *salary*. The field type defines the data type of the keyword. Finally, the pointer *ptr* locates the keyword in the first employee record. This field specifies where the search will begin. For example, if the current task is to search all records to find a salary of 3500.75, *ptr* would contain the address of the field *salary* in the first record of the employee record array.

The following listing demonstrates how the generic search algorithm can be implemented.

```
#include <stdio.h>
#include <stdlib.h>

#define INT 0
#define FLOAT 1
#define STRING 2

struct emp
{
    char name[20] ;
    int age ;
    float salary ;
} ;
struct field
{
    char keyword[20] ;
    int type ;
    struct emp *ptr ;
} ;

search ( int type, struct emp *ptr, struct emp *start,
int len, void *user_value ) ;

typecheck ( struct field *f, struct emp *ptr, int len,
char *user_keyword, char *user_value ) ;
```

```
main( )
{
    struct emp e[ ]= {
                        "Sanjay",23,2455.55, "Sameer",27,3500.75,
                        "Rahul", 34,4500.55, "Rakesh",26,2500.45,
                        "Akshay",22,1700.50
                     } ;
    struct field f[4] = {
                        "name", STRING,NULL, "age",INT,NULL,
                        "salary",FLOAT, NULL, "last",NULL,NULL
                     } ;
    int i, len ;
    char user_keyword[10], user_value[100] ;

    f[0].ptr = ( struct emp * ) &e[0].name ;
    f[1].ptr = ( struct emp * ) &e[0].age ;
    f[2].ptr = ( struct emp * ) &e[0].salary ;

    len = sizeof ( e ) / sizeof ( e[0] ) ;

    strcpy ( user_value, "3500.75" ) ;
    strcpy ( user_keyword, "salary" ) ;

    printf ( "\n\nuser_value = %s", user_value ) ;
    printf ( "\nuser_keyword = %s", user_keyword ) ;

    typecheck ( f, e, len, user_keyword, user_value ) ;

    strcpy ( user_value, "Sanjay" ) ;
    strcpy ( user_keyword, "name" ) ;

    printf ( "\n\nuser_value = %s", user_value ) ;
    printf ( "\nuser_keyword = %s", user_keyword ) ;

    typecheck ( f, e, len, user_keyword, user_value ) ;
```

```c
        strcpy ( user_value, "99" ) ;
        strcpy ( user_keyword,"number" ) ;

        printf ( "\n\nuser_value = %s", user_value ) ;
        printf ( "\nuser_keyword = %s", user_keyword ) ;

        typecheck ( f, e, len, user_keyword, user_value ) ;

        strcpy ( user_value, "40" ) ;
        strcpy ( user_keyword,"age" ) ;

        printf ( "\n\nuser_value = %s",user_value ) ;
        printf ( "\nuser_keyword = %s",user_keyword ) ;

        typecheck ( f, e, len, user_keyword, user_value ) ;
}

typecheck ( struct field *f, struct emp *start, int len,
                    char *user_keyword, char *user_value )
{
        int i ;
        int integer ; /* integer value */
        float floater ; /* float value */
        char *string ; /* string pointer */

        for ( i = 0 ; strcmp ( f[i].keyword, "last" ) != 0 ; i++ )
        {
            if ( strcmp ( f[i].keyword, user_keyword ) == 0 )
                break ;
        }

        if ( strcmp ( f[i].keyword, "last" ) == 0 )
        {
            printf ( "\nError: keyword '%s' not legal.", user_keyword ) ;
            return ;
        }
```

```c
        switch ( f[i].type )
        {
            case INT :
                integer = atoi ( user_value ) ;
                search ( INT, f[i].ptr, start, len, ( void * ) &integer ) ;
                break ;

            case FLOAT:
                floater = atof ( user_value ) ;
                search ( FLOAT, f[i].ptr, start, len, ( void * ) & floater ) ;
                break ;

            case STRING:
                string = user_value ;
                search ( STRING, f[i].ptr, start, len, ( void * ) string ) ;
                break ;
        }
}

search ( int type, struct emp *ptr, struct emp *start,
                int len, void *user_value )
{
        int i ;
        int integer ;
        float floater ;
        char *string ;

        switch ( type )
        {
            case INT :
                for ( i = 0 ; i < len ; i++ )
                {
                    integer = * ( ( int * ) ptr ) ;

                    if ( integer == * ( ( int * ) user_value ) )
                    {
                        display ( &start[i] ) ; return ;
```

```
                    }
                    ptr++ ;
               }
               break ;

          case FLOAT :
               for ( i = 0 ; i < len ; i++ )
               {
                    floater = * ( ( float * ) ptr ) ;

                    if ( floater == * ( ( float * ) user_value ) )
                    {
                         display ( &start[i] ) ; return ;
                    }
                    ptr++ ;
               }
               break ;

          case STRING :
               string = ( char * ) ptr ;

               for ( i = 0 ; i < len ; i++ )
               {
                    if ( strcmp ( string, ( char * ) user_value ) == 0 )
                    {
                         display ( &start[i] ) ; return ;
                    }
                    ptr++ ;
               }
     }

     printf ( "\nNo match" ) ;
}

display ( struct emp *start )
{
     printf ( "\nname = %s age = %d salary = %8.2f", start->name,
```

```
        start->age, start->salary ) ;
        getch( ) ;
}
```

There are two routines at the heart of the search algorithm. The actual search function is *search()*. Because *search()* has no knowledge of the data type that is passed to it, the function *typecheck()* provides this information.

The *typecheck()* function performs two jobs. It determines whether the *user_keyword* passed to it actually exists in the structure definitions or not. If it does not exist, an error occurs. For example, the following query would be illegal:

```
find all hra = 1350.75
```

because *hra* is not a valid keyword. When a match is made, the second function is performed. With the keyword known, the type is easily determined and can be converted to its proper format as shown below.

```
        integer = atoi ( user_value ) ;
        floater = atof ( user_value ) ;
        string = user_value ;
```

At this point, all the information necessary to call *search()* has been determined. The *search()* routine is straightforward. It only requires a compact *switch* statement. The *void* pointer *user_value* represents the search key and provides the mechanism that makes this program independent of the data type of the field on which the search is being carried out.

Since this chapter centers around the search algorithm, the structures are built internally. In any practical application, all the information loaded into the employee record array would be read in from a file. A basic linear search will search the arrays in this program, but any search algorithm would suffice.

# 18 *rm Unix Style*

U nix offers a very powerful utility called *rm* to delete files and/or directories present on the disk. It usually provides the following options:

-i      Inquire before deleting
-r      Recursively delete nested directories
-v      Verbose mode, list files and directories as they are removed
-f      Removes files/directories without prompting

These option flags apply only to those items that follow them on the command line. For example,

     rm myfile.txt -r a:mydir -i a:bpbdir

will delete the file *myfile.txt*, then recursively delete *a:\mydir* and all its contents, then ask before recursively deleting *a:bpbdir*. If you say *yes*, it will then stop on each item in *a:bpbdir* and ask your consent before deleting it. If you leave anything undeleted (i.e. the directory is not empty) then the directory chain down to the leftover items will not be removed even if you asked it to do so. If you respond "no" to removing a directory, that directory and all it's contents are left alone.

The *-i*, option is mutually exclusive with the *-f* option (i.e. each will cancel the other for the items following them on the command line.

Let us now simulate the Unix *rm* command under DOS. The following program shows how this can be done. Note that our *rm* utility does not delete the current directory or the root directory. Also, it doesn't delete directories with anything left in them. Lastly, unlike Unix, to remove everything, you must provide the skeleton "*.*" and not just a "*"

```c
#include "dos.h"
#include "stdio.h"
#include "string.h"
#include "dir.h"

#define TRUE 1
#define FALSE 0

/* default search mask */
#define S_MASK ( FA_HIDDEN I FA_SYSTEM I FA_DIREC )
#define MAXLEN 128  /* length of the DOS command line */

struct ffblk dta ;  /* DOS Data Transfer Area table */
int inquire, recurse, verbose ;  /* option flags */
int name ;  /* flag to see if a name was ever given */

main ( int argc, char *argv[ ] )
{
    inquire = FALSE ;  /* initialize flags */
    recurse = FALSE ;
    verbose = FALSE ;
    name = FALSE ;

    clrscr( ) ;

    if ( argc < 2 )  /* if no arguments, print usage */
        usage( ) ;
```

```
        /* parse the command line */
        check_cmd_line ( argc, argv ) ;

        if ( name == FALSE )
            usage( ) ;  /* if no names given, print usage */
}

check_cmd_line ( int argc, char *argv[ ] )
{
        int i ;
        char *s ;

        for ( i = 1 ; i < argc ; i++ )  /* check the arguments */
        {
            s = argv[i] ;
            if ( *s == '-' )
            {
                s++ ;

                switch ( *s )
                {
                    case 'i' :
                        inquire = TRUE ;
                        break ;

                    case 'r' :
                        recurse = TRUE ;
                        break ;

                    case 'v' :
                        verbose = TRUE ;
                        break ;

                    case 'f' :
                        inquire = FALSE ;
                        break ;
```

```
                    default :
                          printf ( "Invalid option %s\n", argv[i] ) ;
                          usage( ) ;
                    }
              }
              else
              {
                    name = TRUE ;
                    delete ( strupr ( argv[i] ) ) ;
              }
        }
}

usage( )
{
      printf ( "\nUSAGE: rm [-i] [-v] [-f] [-r] file_or_directory_name ( s )\n\n" ) ;
      printf ( " -i Inquire before deleting\n" ) ;
      printf ( " -v List files and directories as they are removed\n" ) ;
      printf ( " -f Remove without prompting\n" ) ;
      printf ( " -r Recursively delete directory structures\n" ) ;

      exit ( 1 ) ;
}

delete ( char *arg )
{
      char dirspec[MAXLEN] ;  /* string to store directory path */
      char *tmp ; int flag ;
      struct ffblk dta ;

      /* strip off the filename part */
      strcpy ( dirspec, arg ) ;

      if ( ( tmp = strrchr ( dirspec, '\\' ) ) == NULL )
      {
            if ( ( tmp = strrchr ( dirspec, ':' ) ) == NULL )
```

```
                    strset ( dirspec, '\0' ) ;
              else
              {
                    tmp++ ;
                    strset ( tmp, '\0' ) ;
              }
        }
        else
        {
              tmp++ ;
              strset ( tmp, '\0' ) ;
        }

        flag = findfirst ( arg, &dta, S_MASK ) ;

        if ( flag == 0 )
        {
              while ( flag == 0 )
              {
                    delitem ( dirspec, &dta ) ;
                    flag = findnext ( &dta ) ;
              }
        }
        else
        {
              if ( verbose == TRUE )
                    printf ( "\n%s NOT FOUND", arg ) ;
        }
}

delitem ( char *arg, struct ffblk *dta )
{
        char spec[MAXLEN], ans ;

        /* don't try to delete the files "." & ".." */
        if ( ( strcmp(dta->ff_name, "." ) != 0 ) &&
              ( strcmp ( dta->ff_name, ".." ) != 0 ) )
```

```
        {
            strcpy ( spec, arg ) ;
            strcat ( spec, dta->ff_name ) ;

            if ( dta->ff_attrib & FA_DIREC )  /* if it is directory */
            {
                if ( recurse )  /* and we wish to remove it */
                {
                    if ( inquire )  /* and we want to ask first */
                    {
                        printf ( "\nRemove directory %s (y/n)?", spec ) ;
                        ans = getche( ) ;

                        if ( toupper ( ans ) == 'Y' )
                            delete_dir ( spec ) ;
                    }
                    else
                        delete_dir ( spec ) ;
                }
            }
            else  /* assume it is a normal file */
            {
                if ( inquire )
                {
                    printf ( "\nRemove file %s ( y/n )? ", spec ) ;
                    ans = getche( ) ;

                    if ( toupper ( ans ) == 'Y' )
                        delete_file ( spec, dta ) ;
                }
                else
                    delete_file ( spec, dta ) ;
            }
        }
    }
}

delete_dir ( char *arg )
```

```
    {
        char tempspec[MAXLEN] ;

        if ( verbose )
            printf ( "\nRemoving directory %s", arg ) ;

        if ( rmdir ( arg ) != 0 )  /* if not empty */
        {
            strcpy ( tempspec, arg ) ;  /* create new search string */
            strcat ( tempspec, "\\*.*" ) ;

            delete ( tempspec ) ;  /* then recurse into it to empty it */

            if ( ( ( rmdir ( arg ) != 0 ) && ( verbose == TRUE ) )
                printf ( "\n%s NOT REMOVED", arg ) ;
        }
    }

    delete_file ( char *arg, struct ffblk *dta )
    {
        char flag ;

        if ( ( ( dta->ff_attrib & FA_RDONLY ) != 0 )
            chmod ( arg, ( dta->ff_attrib & ! ( FA_RDONLY ) ) ) ;
        flag = remove ( arg ) ;

        if ( flag == 0 )
        {
            if ( verbose == TRUE )
                printf ( "\n%s file removed successfully", arg ) ;
        }
        else
        {
            if ( verbose == TRUE )
                printf ( "\n%s NOT REMOVED", arg ) ;
        }
    }
```

The arguments passed to *main()* from command line are passed on
to the function *check_cmd_line()*. This function checks the arguments for option flags that may have been specified and passes the
file/directory names to the function *delete()* for carrying out the actual
deletion.

The *delete()* function expands an item name, possibly containing '*'
or '?' and calls *deleteitem()* to delete all matching files (or directories
if -r is given). The *deleteitem()* function calls either the function
*deletedir()* or *deletefile()* to carry out the deletion job.

# 19 Bresenham's Line Drawing Algorithm

**W**e are required to draw straight lines in a great many computer-generated pictures. Hence it is worthwhile finding out how they are drawn. It is not as simple as it appears to be.

Before we embark upon understanding the line-drawing algorithm let me first remind you about the co-ordinate system in the real world of limited-precision displays. The top left corner of the screen is (0, 0) and $x$ increases horizontally, whereas $y$ increases vertically downwards. Also, any addressable point on the display has an integer $x$ and $y$ co-ordinate. With such a co-ordinate system and a display, drawing a vertical, horizontal or a diagonal line at an angle of 45 degrees is fairly simple.

In case of a horizontal line $x$ co-ordinate should be incremented or decremented by 1, whereas the $y$ co-ordinate remains unchanged. Likewise, in case of a vertical line the $y$ co-ordinate should be incremented or decremented by 1, whereas the x co-ordinate remains unchanged. In case of a 45 degree line depending upon the orientation of the line x is incremented or decremented, and so also is y. Note that as the line progresses at every step x as well as the y co-ordinate changes.

However, if the line is inclined at an angle other than 45 degrees then at each step both x and y may not change. For example, if a line is to be drawn from (0, 0) to (100, 50) as we start drawing from (0, 0), x would change more frequently as compared to y since the x distance is the predominant distance. That is, we have to travel more units along x-axis as compared to the y-axis. In such situations x is incremented at every step whereas the algorithm decides whether or not y should be incremented at a given step. Likewise, if for some other line the y distance is the predominant distance then y is incremented at each step whereas x may or may not be.

An interesting algorithm has been developed by Bresenham which changes one of the coordinate value by 1 at each iteration. The other coordinate may or may not change, depending on the value of an error term maintained by the algorithm. This error term records the distance, measured perpendicular to the axis of greatest movement, between the exact path of the line and the actual dots generated. Let us understand this algorithm in detail.

The slope of the line m is given by

$$m = dely / delx$$

where,

$$dely = y_b - y_a$$
$$delx = x_b - x_a$$

Naturally, m can be any real number. To simplify our discussion, we will first consider a line for which $x_a < x_b$ and the slope of the line lies between 0 and 1. In this case, as x increases from $x_a$ to $x_b$, the corresponding $y$ increases from $y_a$ to $y_b$, but $y$ increases less rapidly than does $x$ because *delx* > *dely*. As $x$ increases in unit increments from $x_a$ to $x_b$, the best integer $y$ value will sometimes stay the same and sometimes increment by one. Bresenham's algorithm quickly determines which of these should occur. Note that $y$ need never either decrement or increment by more than 1.

The following figure represents a portion of the line under consideration. Each intersection in the grid represents the center of a pixel.

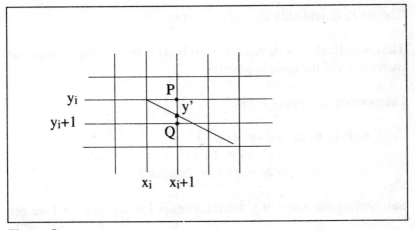

Figure 5

Assume that at $x_i$ the best y-value is $y_i$. We wish to know whether the line at $x_{i+1}$ is closer to the point $P_i = (x_i, y_i)$ or to $Q_i = (x_i, y_i+1)$. At $x_i$ the ideal line has y-value given by,

$$y' = m(x_i - x_a) + y_a \text{ ---- Equation 1}$$

Bresenham used the following measures of the error between the candidate points and the ideal line at $x_i$:

$$e(P_i) = y' - y_i$$
$$e(Q_i) = (y_i + 1) - y' \text{ ---- Equation 2}$$

For the ideal line shown in the figure, both of these errors are positive, and $e(P_i)$ would be less than $e(Q_i)$ if the line passes closer to $P_i$ than to $Q_i$.

One possible position of the ideal line is shown in the figure. However, it is quite possible that it passes slightly below $Q_i$ or slightly above $P_i$. If the line passes below $Q_i$, the error $e(Q_i)$ becomes negative, and if it passes above $P_i$, the error $e(P_i)$ becomes negative. In all of these cases the difference, $e(P_i) - e(Q_i)$, can be used to determine which candidate is closer, using the following rule:

Choose $P_i$ if, and only if, $e(P_i) - e(Q_i) < 0$.

Thus, we should not increment $y$ if this error term is negative and do increment $y$ if the error is positive.

Let us evaluate $e(P_i) - e(Q_i)$.

$$\begin{aligned}
e(P_i) - e(Q_i) &= y' - y_i - ((y_i + 1) - y') \\
&= y' - y_i - y_i - 1 + y' \\
&= 2y' - 2y_i - 1 \quad \text{---- Equation 3}
\end{aligned}$$

Substituting the value of $y'$ from Equation 1 into Equation 3 we get,

$$\begin{aligned}
e(P_i) - e(Q_i) &= 2(m(x_i - x_a) + y_a) - 2y_i - 1 \\
&= 2(m(x_i - x_a) + 2(y_a - y_i) - 1 \quad \text{---- Equation 4}
\end{aligned}$$

Here, the only non-integer number is $m$, which is equal to the ratio of two positive integers, *dely* and *delx*. Multiply Equation 4 by *delx* (which won't change the sign of the error, as $delx > 0$) to form the final error measure $e_i$:

$$\begin{aligned}
e_i &= delx(e(P_i) - e(Q_i)) \\
&= 2\,dely(x_i - x_a) + 2\,delx(y_a - y_i) - delx \quad \text{---- Equation 5}
\end{aligned}$$

Thus the decision rule is, if $e_i < 0$, then choose $y_i = y_i$, otherwise choose $y_i = y_i + 1$.

To see how to iterate with this test, Equation 5 can be written in terms of $e_{i+1}$ by just replacing $i$ by $i+1$ everywhere to obtain,

$$e_{i+1} = 2 \text{ dely } ( x_{i+1} - x_a ) + 2 \text{ delx } ( y_a - y_{i+1} ) - \text{delx}$$

We can write $e_{i+1}$ in terms of $e_i$ to get the amount by which the error term must be updated at each step:

$$e_{i+1} - e_i = 2 \text{ dely } ( x_{i+1} - x_a ) + 2 \text{ delx } ( y_a - y_{i+1} ) - \text{delx}$$
$$- ( 2 \text{ dely } ( x_i - x_a ) + 2 \text{ delx } ( y_a - y_i ) - \text{delx} )$$
$$= 2 \text{ dely } ( x_{i+1} - x_i ) - 2 \text{ delx } ( y_{i+1} - y_i )$$

Recognize that for the line under consideration $x_{i+1} - x_i = 1$, hence the above equation becomes,

$$e_{i+1} = e_i + 2 \text{ dely } - 2 \text{ delx } ( y_{i+1} - y_i ) \text{ ---- Equation 6}$$

So at each stop on the way from $x_a$ to $x_b$ we test the sign of $e_i$, choose $y_i$ accordingly, and then compute the next error term, $e_{i+1}$. If $y$ is not incremented, then $y_i = y_{i+1}$, and from Equation 6 $e_{i+1} = e_i + 2 \text{ } dely$. If $y$ is incremented then $e_{i+1} = e_i + 2 ( \text{ } dely - delx)$.

Let us now see how to start the process at $i = 0$. Now $x_0 = x_a$ and $y_0 = y_a$. Thus, according to Equation 5, with $i = 1$ we get

$$e1 = 2 * \text{ dely } - \text{delx}$$

The algorithm that we have discussed copes only with the special case $x_a < x_b$ and $0 < m < 1$.

The following table shows the other cases and the relevant parameters for each case.

| Slope of line | Predominant distance | Coord. which changes at each step | Coord. which may or may not change |
|---|---|---|---|
| 0 < m < 1 | x | x | y |
| m = 1 | x or y | x and y | - |
| 1 < m < 0 | y | y | x |
| 0 > m > -1 | x | x | y |
| m = -1 | x or y | x and y | - |
| -1 > m > 0 | y | y | x |

Figure 6

Given below is the code for implementing Bresenham's algorithm for all cases mentioned in the Figure 6. The error term for each case can be derived on similar lines as discussed above.

```c
#include "graphics.h"

#define INCR 1
#define DECR -1
#define PREDX 1
#define PREDY 0

int dx, dy, e, e_inc, e_noinc ;

main( )
{
    int gd = DETECT, gm ;

    initgraph ( &gd, &gm, "c:\\tc\\bgi" ) ;

    bressline ( 0, 300, 300, 300 ) ; /* m = 0, horizontal line */
    bressline ( 100, 200, 100, 300 ) ; /* m = infinity, vertical line */
    bressline ( 0, 0, 100, 50 ) ; /* 0 < m < 1 */
```

```
        bressline ( 100, 50, 0, 0 ) ; /* 0 < m < 1 */
        bressline ( 0, 0, 100, 100 ) ; /* m = 1 */
        bressline ( 100, 100, 0, 0 ) ; /* m = 1 */
        bressline ( 0, 0, 100, 150 ) ; /* 1 < m < infinity */
        bressline ( 100, 150, 0, 0 ) ; /* 1 < m < infinity */
        bressline ( 0, 150, 100, 100 ) ; /* 0 > m > -1 */
        bressline ( 100, 100, 0, 150 ) ; /* 0 > m > -1 */
        bressline ( 0, 200, 100, 100 ) ; /* m = -1 */
        bressline ( 100, 100, 0, 200 ) ; /* m = -1 */
        bressline ( 100, 100, 0, 300 ) ; /* -1 > m > 0 */
        bressline ( 0, 300, 100, 100 ) ; /* -1 > m > 0 */

        getch( ) ;
        closegraph( ) ;
}

bressline ( int x1, int y1, int x2, int y2 )
{
        int incdec, t, i ;

        if ( x1 > x2 )
        {
                t = x1 ;
                x1 = x2 ;
                x2 = t ;

                t = y1 ;
                y1 = y2 ;
                y2 = t ;
        }

        dx = x2 - x1 ;
        dy = y2 - y1 ;

        if ( dx == 0 )  /* vertical line */
        {
                if ( y1 > y2 )
```

```
        {
            t = y1 ;
            y1 = y2 ;
            y2 = t ;
        }

        for ( i = y1 ; i <= y2 ; i++ )
            putpixel ( x1, i, WHITE ) ;

        return ;
    }

    if ( dy == 0 )  /* horizontal line */
    {
        for ( i = x1 ; i < x2 ; i++ )
            putpixel ( i, y1, WHITE ) ;

        return ;
    }

    /* 0 < m < 1 */
    if ( dy < dx && dy > 0 )
    {
        e_noinc = 2 * dy ;
        e = 2 * dy - dx ;
        e_inc = 2 * ( dy - dx ) ;

        drawline ( x1, y1, x2, y2, PREDX, INCR ) ;
    }

    /* m = 1 */
    if ( dy == dx && dy > 0 )
    {
        e_noinc = 2 * dy ;
        e = 2 * dy - dx ;
        e_inc = 2 * ( dy - dx ) ;
```

```c
        drawline ( x1, y1, x2, y2, PREDX, INCR ) ;
}

/* 1 < m < infinity */
if ( dy > dx && dy > 0 )
{
    e_noinc = 2 * dx ;
    e = 2 * dx - dy ;
    e_inc = 2 * ( dx - dy ) ;

    drawline ( x1, y1, x2, y2, PREDY, INCR ) ;
}

/* 0 > m > -1 */
if ( -dy < dx && dy < 0 )
{
    dy = -dy ;
    e_noinc = 2 * dy ;
    e = 2 * dy - dx ;
    e_inc = 2 * ( dy - dx ) ;

    drawline ( x1, y1, x2, y2, PREDX, DECR ) ;
}

/* m = -1 */
if ( dy == -dx && dy < 0 )
{
    dy = -dy ;
    e_noinc = ( 2 * dy ) ;
    e = 2 * dy - dx ;
    e_inc = 2 * ( dy - dx ) ;

    drawline ( x1, y1, x2, y2, PREDX, DECR ) ;
}

/* -1 > m > 0 */
if ( -dy > dx && dy < 0 )
```

```
        {
             dx = -dx ;
             e_noinc = - ( 2 * dx ) ;
             e = 2 * dx - dy ;
             e_inc = - 2 * ( dx - dy ) ;

             drawline ( x2, y2, x1, y1, PREDY, DECR ) ;
        }
}

drawline ( int x1, int y1, int x2, int y2, int pred, int incdec )
{
     int i, start, end, var ;

     if ( pred == PREDX )
     {
          start = x1 ;
          end = x2 ;
          var = y1 ;
     }
     else
     {
          start = y1 ;
          end = y2 ;
          var = x1 ;
     }
     for ( i = start ; i <= end ; i++ )
     {
          if ( pred == PREDY )
               putpixel ( var, i, WHITE ) ;
          else
               putpixel ( i, var, WHITE ) ;

          if ( e < 0 )
               e += e_noinc ;
          else
          {
```

```
        var += incdec ;
        e += e_inc ;
      }
    }
  }
```

# 20

# *Bresenham's* *Circle Drawing* *Algorithm*

I n the last chapter we saw how to draw lines at any angle. Circles too are frequently needed in applications, and we need a way to generate their corresponding pixel patterns from the information such as coordinates of the center and the radius. Let us first see the theory behind the Bresenham's circle generating algorithm.

Suppose we want to draw a circle with center (0,0) and radius $R$, where $R$ is an integer. We want the set of pixels that should be lit up to provide the best approximation to the ideal circle. The equation of a circle is $X^2 + Y^2 = R^2$.

But we can reduce the amount of computation required by capitalising on the symmetry of a circle, as we need only compute the $(x,y)$ values in one octant of the circle. For a given point $(x,y)$ on the circle there are seven other points along the circle whose coordinates can be easily found. Simply negating and/or interchanging $x$ and $y$

produces the seven locations, $(-x,y)$, $(-x,-y)$, $(x,-y)$, $(y,x)$, $(-y,x)$, $(-y,-x)$ and $(y,-x)$. This is shown in the following figure.

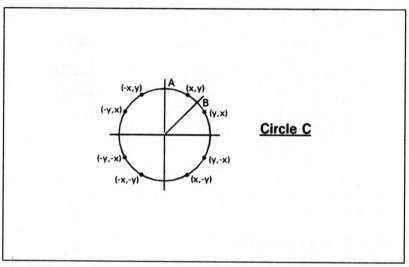

Figure 7

Assuming that the coordinates of the pixel to be illuminated in the octant A to B are $P(x,y)$. $P$ should lie at distance $R$ from the origin, so a measure of the error exhibited by $P$ can be the difference between the square of its true distance and $R^2$:

$$e(P) = (x^2 + y^2) - R^2$$

Error $e(P)$ will be positive if $P$ is too far from the origin, and negative otherwise.

Suppose we have determined that the best point at step $i$ is $P_i = (x_i, y_i)$. Now we can increment $x_i$ by 1 and ask which of the points, $S_i=(x_i +1, y_i)$ or $T_i=(x_i + 1, y_i-1)$, is closer to the circle. We can form the errors $e(S_i)$ and $e(T_i)$ for these candidates, but we want to find a way to combine them into a single error quantity, say $d_i$, whose sign then can be used to make the choice between the two points.

*C Pearls*

The three cases that can occur are shown in the following figure.

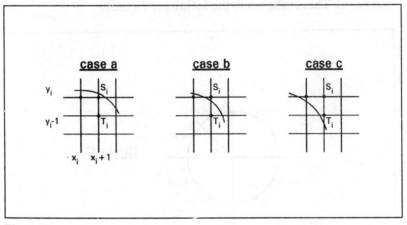

Figure 8

Let us tackle the three cases:

(a)    The (true) circle C lies between $S_i$ and $T_i$. If $C$ lies between the two points, the two errors will have opposite signs: $e(S_i) > 0$, whereas $e(T_i) < 0$. We can use the sign of their sum as the error quantity: $d_i = e(S_i) + e(T_i)$. If $C$ is nearer $T_i$ the sum $d_i$ will be positive. On the other hand, if $S_i$ is closer to $C$, the sum will be negative. So the test: "Choose $S_i$ if $d_i < 0$; otherwise choose $T_i$ works for this case.

(b)    If the true circle lies above (or on) $S_i$ we should choose $S_i$ as both errors are negative, and so their sum $d_i$ is negative. Thus the same test would work.

(c)    If the true circle lies below (or on) $T_i$. Here $T_i$ must be chosen, since $d_i$ is positive because both errors are positive.

Thus we can now frame the rule for all three cases: "Choose $S_i$ if $d_i < 0$; otherwise choose $T_i$".

Now what remains to be done is finding an efficient way to update $d_i$.

We have found that the error term $d_i$ is equal to:

$$d_i = e(S_i) + e(T_i)$$
$$= 2(x_i + 1)^2 + y_{i2} + (y_i - 1)^2 - 2R^2$$

Likewise,

$$d_{i+1} = 2[(x_i + 1) + 1]^2 + y_{i+1}^2 + (y_{i+1} - 1)^2 - 2R^2$$

Writing $d_{i+1}$ in terms of $d_i$ we get:

$$d_{i+1} = d_i + 4x_i + 6 + 2(y_{i+1}^2 - y_i^2) - 2(y_{i+1} - y_i)$$

If $d_{i+1} < 0$ then $y$ does not change and $d_{i+1}$ is:

$$d_{i+1} = d_i + 4x_i + 6$$

Otherwise $y_{i+1} = y_{i-1}$ and $d_{i+1}$ is:

$$d_{i+1} = d_i + 4(x_i - y_i) + 10$$

To start the algorithm, $X_0 = 0$ and $y_0 = R$ hence

$$S_i = (1, R)$$

and

$$T_i = (1, R - 1).$$

Thus, $d_i = 3 - 2R$.

If we are to draw the circle of radius $R$ placed at center point $(x_c, y_c)$, the circle is shifted to this center simply by offsetting the $x$ and $y$ values as shown in the following program:

```
# include "graphics.h"
main( )
{
    int i, j, x1, y1, r, p, a ;
    int gd, gm = DETECT, x, y ;

    initgraph ( &gm, &gd, "c:\\tc\\bgi" ) ;

    printf ( "\nEnter coordinates of center and radius of circle" ) ;
    scanf ( "%d%d%d", &x, &y, &r ) ;

    x1 = 0 ;
    y1 = r ;
    p = 3 - 2 * r ;

    while ( x1 < y1 )
    {
        plotcircle ( x, y, x1, y1 ) ;

        if ( p < 0 )
            p = p + 4 * x1 + 6 ;
        else
        {
            p = p + 4 * ( x1 - y1 ) + 10 ;
            y1 = y1 - 1 ;
        }

        x1 = x1 + 1 ;

    }

    if ( x1 == y1 )
        plotcircle ( x, y, x1, y1 ) ;

    getch( ) ;
    closegraph( ) ;
    restorecrtmode( ) ;
```

```
}

plotcircle ( int x, int y, int x1, int y1 )
{
    putpixel ( x + x1, y + y1, 15 ) ;
    putpixel ( x - x1, y + y1, 15 ) ;
    putpixel ( x + x1, y - y1, 15 ) ;
    putpixel ( x - x1, y - y1, 15 ) ;
    putpixel ( x + y1, y + x1, 15 ) ;
    putpixel ( x - y1, y + x1, 15 ) ;
    putpixel ( x + y1, y - x1, 15 ) ;
    putpixel ( x - y1, y - x1, 15 ) ;
}
```

# 21 *The Fractal Magic*

The term fractal has become widely associated in graphics with randomly generated curves and surfaces that exhibit a degree of self-similarity. Nature provides examples that mimic self-similarity. Fractals are used to provide "naturalistic" shapes for representing objects such as coast-lines, rugged mountains, grass, and fire.

The concept of fractals is an idea of Benoit Mandelbrot of the IBM Research Center who pioneered investigations into the nature of self-similarity. He developed and popularized the field of fractals virtually single-handedly. Mandelbrot calls various forms of self-similar curves 'fractals' short for "fractional dimensional". A line is one dimensional and a plane is two dimensional, but a curve of infinite length that fits into a finite region of the plane must have a dimension somewhere between 1 and 2. Accordingly, Mandelbrot devised a method for computing the fractional dimension for such curves.

In this chapter we intend to explore Fractal Trees. A fractalization process can be used to generate shapes that resemble a tree. The definition of a tree here is inherently recursive: A tree is a branch with several trees emanating from the end of the branch. Thus at the end of each branch another smaller set of branches is produced, and at the end of each of its branches yet another set is produced. This can be easily implemented through a recursive routine that calls itself until a certain depth of recursion is reached. Thus one can draw "third-order trees," "fourth-order trees," and so on.

To organise the logic of tree generation consider the following figure.

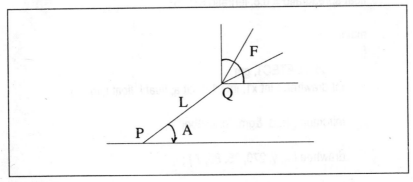

Figure 9

The branch of the tree begins at point $P$ and extends for a length $L$ at an angle $A$ degrees, terminating at point $Q$. At $Q$ a new tree is produced, with *numbranch* branches distributed over an angle (known as spread-out angle) of $F$ degrees. To allow branches in trees to get shorter (or longer) at successive stages, the parameter *lengthratio* is used, which specifies the ratio of the length of a branch to that of its parent branch. Similarly, *spreadratio* is the ratio of the spread-out angle in a tree relative to that in its parent tree.

The program given below uses this approach to draw a tree. The routine *drawtree( )* is invoked as

```
drawtree ( start, 90.0, len, spreadoutangle, order )
```

The recursion stops when the specified depth is reached. Referring Figure 9 given above would help you to understand the logic better.

```c
#include "graphics.h"
#include "math.h"
#include "stdlib.h"
#define rads 0.0174  /* 3.14/180 */

int x = 280, y = 350, numbranch = 3 ;
float spreadratio = 0.8, lenratio = 0.75 ;

main( )
{
    int gd = DETECT, gm ;
    int drawtree ( int x1, int y1, float a, float l, float f, int n ) ;

    initgraph ( &gd, &gm, "c:\\tc\\bgi" ) ;

    drawtree ( x, y, 270, 75, 80, 7 ) ;

    getch( ) ;
    closegraph( ) ;
    restorecrtmode( ) ;
}

drawtree ( int x1, int y1, float a, float l, float f, int n )
{
    int i, num, x2, y2 ;
    float delang, ang ;

    if ( n > 0 )
    {
        x2 = x1 + l * cos ( rads * a ) ;
        y2 = y1 + l * sin ( rads * a ) ;

        setcolor ( WHITE ) ;
        line ( x1, y1, x2, y2 ) ;
```

```
    num  = numbranch ;

    if ( num > 1 )
        delang = f / ( num - 1.0 ) ;
    else
        delang = 0.0 ;

    ang = a - f / 2.0 - delang ;
    for ( i = 1 ; i <= num ; i++ )
    {
        ang += delang ;
        drawtree ( x2, y2, ang, l * lenratio, f * spreadratio, n - 1 ) ;
    }
}
else
{
    setcolor ( random ( 7 ) + 1 ) ;
    ellipse ( x2, y2, 0, 276, 2, 4 ) ;
    fillellipse ( x2, y2, 2, 4 ) ;
}
}
```

# 22 *Fractal Trees*

In the last chapter we saw how to use the fractalization process to generate shapes that resemble a tree. To reiterate the idea - the definition of a fractal tree is inherently recursive: A tree is a branch with several trees emanating from the end of the branch. Thus at the end of each branch another smaller set of branches is produced, and at the end of each of its branches yet another set is produced. This can be easily implemented through a recursive routine that calls itself until a certain depth of recursion is reached. The tree that we drew in the last chapter was of uniform shape - a rare phenomenon in real life. A tree would look more natural if some of its parameters like number of branches or spreadout angle are varied randomly in each recursive call. The following program shows how this can be achieved. Referring Figure 9 from Chapter 21 would help you to understand the logic better.

```
# include "graphics.h"
# include "math.h"
# include "stdlib.h"

# define rads 0.0174  /* 3.14/180 */
```

```
int x = 280, y = 350, numbranch = 3 ;
float spreadratio = 0.5, lenratio = 1.0 ;

main( )
{
    int gd = DETECT, gm ;
    int drawtree ( int x1, int y1, float a, float l, float f, int n ) ;

    initgraph ( &gd, &gm, "c:\\tc\\bgi" ) ;
    drawtree ( x, y, 270, 50, 90, 6 ) ;
    getch( ) ;
    closegraph( ) ;
    restorecrtmode( ) ;
}

drawtree ( int x1, int y1, float a, float l, float f, int n )
{
    int i, num, color, x2, y2 ;
    float delang, ang ;

    if ( n > 0 )
    {
        switch ( n )
        {
            case 1:
                setcolor ( LIGHTGREEN ) ;
                break ;

            case 2:
                setcolor ( GREEN ) ;
                break ;

            case 3:
                setcolor ( RED ) ;
                break ;

            case 4:
```

```
                    setcolor ( BROWN ) ;
                    break ;

              default:
                    setcolor ( DARKGRAY ) ;
        }

        x2 = x1 + l * cos ( rads * a ) ;
        y2 = y1 + l * sin ( rads * a ) ;

        for ( i = 0 ; i < n ; i++ )
        {
            line ( x1 + i, y1, x2 + i, y2 ) ;
            line ( x1 - i, y1, x2 - i, y2 ) ;
        }

        num = random ( 6 ) + 1 ;

        if ( num > 1 )
            delang = f / ( num - 1.0 ) ;
        else
            delang = 0.0 ;

        ang = a - f / 2.0 - delang ;
        for ( i = 1 ; i <= num ; i++ )
        {
            ang += delang ;
            drawtree ( x2, y2, ang + 10, l * lenratio, 1.0 *
                        random ( 90 ) + 1, n - 1 ) ;
        }
    }
    else
    {
        setfillstyle ( SOLID_FILL, random ( 15 ) ) ;
        fillellipse ( x1, y1, 3, 6 ) ; /* drawing fruits */
    }
}
```

# 23 *Inexact String Comparisons*

requently, we like to search a database for a record whose contents we know only approximately. For example, you may want to search a database for a name which you vaguely remember is either Jones, John or Jonathan. In such cases we must be able to perform inexact alphanumeric searches. Moreover, a small typographical error in the word being searched shouldn't give you a "record- not-found" error message. Instead, you should get a number of records, from which you can select the right one. To include such a behavior into your application, you must determine to what extent two character strings differ. One measure comes from comparing the phonetics of both strings. Another approach is to use what is known as 'Levenstein Distance'.

The Levenstein algorithm determines how many mutations are needed to transform string1 into string2. Three types of mutation are possible:

-   addition of a character (if string1 is shorter than string2)
-   deletion of a character (if string1 is longer than string2)
-   changing a character (if characters compared don't match)

Each of these mutations is assigned an individual penalty value. The Levenstein algorithm arrives at a final penalty value by adding all penalties for each required mutation. A final score of zero denotes two equal strings. The higher the score, the more the strings differ. The following program implements this algorithm.

```
#include <stdlib.h>
#include <string.h>
#include <stdio.h>


/* maximum character that should be compared */
#define MAXLEN      20
#define ARR_SIZE     MAXLEN + 1
#define ZERO_IF_EQUAL(x,y) ( string1[x-1] == string2[y-1] ? 0 :
                                        change )

int addition = 0 ;
int change   = 1 ;
int deletion = 2 ;
int distance[ARR_SIZE][ARR_SIZE] ;

main ( int argc, char *argv[] )
{
    int result ;

    if ( argc != 3 )
    {
        printf ( "\nUsage:  LD string1  string2\n" ) ;
        printf ( "\nwhere string1 and string2 are the two strings" ) ;
        printf ( "\nto be compared with the Levenstein distance algorithm." ) ;
        exit ( 1 ) ;
    }
    else
    {
        printf ( "\nComparing '%s' and '%s': \n", argv[1], argv[2] ) ;
        result = lev_dist ( argv[1], argv[2] ) ;
        printf ( "\nResult = %d\n", result ) ;
```

```
        }
    }

    int lev_dist ( char *string1, char *string2 )
    {
        int i, j, len1, len2 ;

        len1 = ( strlen ( string1 ) > MAXLEN ? MAXLEN : strlen ( string1 ) ) ;
        len2 = ( strlen ( string2 ) > MAXLEN ? MAXLEN : strlen ( string2 ) ) ;

        distance[0][0] = 0 ;
        for ( j = 1 ; j <= ARR_SIZE ; j++ )
            distance[0][j] = distance [0][j-1] + addition ;

        for ( j = 1 ; j <= ARR_SIZE ; j++ )
            distance[j][0] = distance[j-1][0] + deletion ;

        for ( i = 1 ; i <= len1 ; i++ )
        {
            for ( j = 1 ; j <= len2 ; j++ )
            distance[i][j] = least ( distance[i-1][j-1] + ZERO_IF_EQUAL(i,j),
                            distance[i][j-1]  + addition,
                            distance[i-1][j]  + deletion ) ;
        }

        printf ( "\n" ) ;
        for ( i = 1 ; i <= ien1 ; i++ )
        {
            for ( j = 1 ; j <= len2 ; j++ )
                printf ( " %3d", distance[i][j] ) ;
            printf ( "\n" ) ;
        }

        return ( distance [len1][len2] ) ;
    }

    least ( int x, int y, int z )
```

```
{
    if ( x < y )
        return ( min ( x, z ) ) ;
    else
        return ( min ( y, z ) ) ;
}
```

The top row of the *distance* array is filled with penalty values for the addition mutation. The leftmost column is filled with penalty values for the deletion mutation. The nested *for* loops fill the distance array with the appropriate values. The bottom right corner of the array contains the final score, the Levenstein Distance. This integer value is returned to the calling routine. Using different strings you can verify that Levenstein Distance increases with increasingly differing strings. Usually, Levenstein Distances for sufficiently similar strings turns out to be below 10. Try changing the values of the variables *addition*, *deletion* and *change* for different sets of strings.

Let us now try to use the Levenstein Distance in a more practical manner. We can use the following logic to either accept or reject a string:

(a)   Compare the first character of both strings by ignoring their cases. If there is a mismatch the string is to be rejected.

(b)   If first character matches, calculate the maximum allowable difference (threshold) using the formula *1+((strlen( string1)+2) | 4)*. If the absolute value of the length difference between the two strings is greater than the threshold value the string should be rejected.

(c)   Calculate the Levenstein Distance. If this value is smaller than or equal to the threshold value the string is accepted. If the calculated distance is larger than the threshold value, the string is rejected.

These steps are implemented by the following program.

```c
#include <stdlib.h>
#include <string.h>
#include <math.h>
#include <ctype.h>
#include <stdio.h>

#define MAXLEN   20
#define ARR_SIZE MAXLEN + 1
#define TU(x) toupper(x)
#define ZERO_IF_EQUAL(x,y) (TU(string1[x-1]) == TU(string2[y-1]) ?
                                          0 : change)
#define OK      1
#define NOTOK 0

int add = 0, change = 1, delete = 2 ;
int distance[ARR_SIZE][ARR_SIZE] ;

main ( int argc, char *argv[ ] )
{
    int result ;

    if ( argc != 3 )
    {
        printf ( "\nUsage: LD string1 string2\n" ) ;
        printf ( "\nwhere string1 and string2 are the two strings" ) ;
        printf ( "\nto be compared with the Levenstein distance algorithm." ) ;
        exit ( 1 ) ;
    }
    else
    {
        printf ( "\nComparing '%s' and '%s': \n", argv[1], argv[2] ) ;
        result = check ( argv[1], argv[2] ) ;
        if ( result == OK )
            printf ( "\nstrings are similar" ) ;
        else
```

```
                printf ( "\nstrings differing too much" ) ;
        }
}

check ( char *string1, char *string2 )
{
    int i, j, len1, len2, threshold ;

    if ( toupper ( *string1 ) != toupper ( *string2 ) )
    {
        printf ( "\nMismatch in first character\n" ) ;
        return ( NOTOK ) ;
    }

    len1 = ( strlen ( string1 ) > MAXLEN ? MAXLEN : strlen ( string1 ) ) ;
    len2 = ( strlen ( string2 ) > MAXLEN ? MAXLEN : strlen ( string2 ) ) ;
    threshold = ( int ) floor ( ( double ) 1 + ( ( len1 + 2 ) / 4 ) ) ;

    if ( abs ( len1 - len2 ) > threshold )
    {
        printf ( "\nRejected due to large length difference \n" ) ;
        return ( NOTOK ) ;
    }

    distance[0][0] = 0 ;
    for ( j = 1 ; j <= ARR_SIZE ; j++ )
        distance[0][j] = distance [0][j-1] + add ;

    for ( j = 1 ; j <= ARR_SIZE ; j++ )
        distance[j][0] = distance[j-1][0] + delete ;

    for ( i = 1 ; i <= len1 ; i++ )
    {
        for ( j = 1 ; j <= len2 ; j++ )
            distance[i][j] = least ( distance[i-1][j-1] + ZERO_IF_EQUAL ( i,j ) ,
                                distance[i][j-1] + add,
                                distance[i-1][j] + delete ) ;
```

```
    }

    printf ( "\nlevenstein distance is %d\n", distance[len1][len2] ) ;
    if ( distance [len1][len2] <= threshold )
        return ( OK ) ;
    else
        return ( NOTOK ) ;
}

least ( int x, int y, int z )
{
    if ( x < y )
        return ( min ( x, z ) ) ;
    else
        return ( min ( y, z ) ) ;
}
```

# 24 *Redirecting*
## *Standard*
## *Errors*

S uppose we wish to execute a program/command at the DOS prompt. If during execution of this program/command an error occurs then the error messages are displayed on the screen, the standard error device. If we want that instead of displaying these error messages on the screen they should be redirected to a file then it can be implemented as shown in the following program.

```
#include "stdio.h"
#include "dos.h"
#include "string.h"
#include "process.h"

main ( int argc, char *argv[] )
{
    int i, fs ;
    char cmdtoexecute[80] ;
    char far ( filename[66] ) ;
```

```
clrscr( ) ;
if ( argc < 2 )
{
    printf ( "\nUsage: %s filename command", argv[0] ) ;
    printf ( "\nfilename = Name of file to send to STDERR output to") ;
    printf ( "\ncommand = Command to execute") ;
    exit ( 1 ) ;
}

strcpy ( cmdtoexecute, argv[2] ) ;
for ( i = 3 ; i < argc ; i++ )
{
    strcat ( cmdtoexecute, " " ) ;
    strcat ( cmdtoexecute, argv[i] ) ;
}

strcpy ( filename, argv[1] ) ;
if ( ( ( fileopen ( filename, &fs ) ) != 0 )
{
    printf ( "File open error" ) ;
    exit ( 2 ) ;
}

if ( ( ( filecopy ( fs ) ) != 0 )
{
    fileclose ( fs ) ;
    printf ( "Cannot force duplicate of STDERR" ) ;
    exit ( 3 ) ;
}
else
{
    system ( cmdtoexecute ) ;
    if ( fileclose ( fs ) != 0 )
    {
        printf ( "File handle close error" ) ;
        exit ( 4 ) ;
```

```
            }
        }
    }

    fileopen ( char far ( *filename ), int *fs )
    {
        union REGS i, o ;
        struct SREGS s ;

        i.h.ah = 0x3c ;
        i.x.cx = 0 ;
        s.ds = FP_SEG ( filename ) ;
        i.x.dx = FP_OFF ( filename ) ;
        intdosx ( &i, &o, &s ) ;
        *fs = o.x.ax ;

        return ( o.x.cflag ) ;
    }

    filecopy ( int fs )
    {
        union REGS i, o ;
        i.h.ah = 0x46 ;
        i.x.bx = fs ;
        i.x.cx = 2 ;
        intdos ( &i, &o ) ;

        return ( o.x.cflag ) ;
    }

    fileclose ( int fs )
    {
        union REGS i, o ;
        i.h.ah = 0x3E ;
        i.x.bx = fs ;
        intdos ( &i, &o ) ;
```

```
        return ( o.x.cflag ) ;
    }
```

# 25 *Changing*
## *Border Colours*

O nce I came across a problem with a software which set the hardware border (overscan area) to a certain colour and did not reset it upon exit. That's the time I started wondering how the border colours can be changed. Given below is a program which uses the BIOS routine, Interrupt 0x10, to change this colour to a user specified value.

The program presented here is CGA compatible which means it will accept input from 0-15. You can modify the same so that a value of 0-63 may be used for EGA/VGA compatible monitors.

You can invoke the program in two ways:.

(a)   By specifying the border with it's argument on the command line, for example, border 0, which will set the border colour to black.

(b)   Without specifying any arguments, in which case you will get a list of the 0-15 colours the border may be set to and a prompt for the value you wish to set the border to.

Here is the program...

```
#include <stdio.h>
#include <dos.h>

/* MXCOLOR defines the maximum color the border can be set to. For
   a CGA and compatible this is 15 while for an EGA/VGA it is 63. */
#define MXCOLOR 15

main ( int argc, char *argv[ ] )
{
    int brd_color=0, delay, i, j;

    if ( argc <= 1 )
    {
        puts ( "\nEnter a number from 0-15 indicating which border" ) ;
        puts ( "\ncolor you wish to use. The results will vary " ) ;
        puts ( "\ndepending on how software has set up the color" ) ;
        puts ( "\npallette but here's how they correspond on a PC/AT486" ) ;
        puts ( "\nwith VGA, in 80 column text mode, and the default pallette:" )
;

        puts ( "\n  0 - Black    5 - Purple    10 - Bright Green 15 - Light Cyan" ) ;
        puts ( "\n  1 - Blue     6 - Yellow    11 - Light Cyan" ) ;
        puts ( "\n  2 - Green    7 - White     12 - Orange" ) ;
        puts ( "\n  3 - Cyan     8 - Dark Green 13 - Purple" ) ;
        puts ( "\n  4 - Red      9 - Light Blue 14 - Green" ) ;
        puts ( "\nChoice: " ) ;
        scanf ( "%d", &brd_color ) ;
    }
    else
    {
        sscanf ( argv[1], "%d", &brd_color ) ;
        bord_change ( brd_color ) ;
    }

    while ( brd_color < 0 || brd_color > MXCOLOR )
    {
```

```
        printf ( "\nInvalid entry! Please enter a number between 0 and 15: " ) ;
        scanf ( "%d", &brd_color ) ;
    }

    bord_change ( brd_color ) ;
    return ( 1 ) ;
}

bord_change ( int colour )
{
    union REGS i, o ;

    i.h.ah = 0x0B ;
    i.x.bx = colour ;
    int86 ( 0x10, &i, &o ) ;
}
```

# 26 *Modifying Search Path*

Here I am presenting a program which modifies the working path for MS-DOS environments by prepending ("-p") or appending ("-a") a new path to an existing path environment. This program operates on the PARENT process environment, thus eliminating the requirement to use a batch file or enter a complete new path specification to make minor modifications to the working path. The program copies the environment block from the parent process to local strings, modifies the local string for PATH, then copies the complete set of environment strings back to the parent environment block.

The program reports an error and leaves the path unmodified if there is insufficient room in the environment block for the modified PATH environment variable. In this situation, the path could not be modified even at the command level. It also reports an error if an invalid switch is given, or if switches are not prefixed with '-'. Here is the program...

```
/* modipath.c */

#include <stdio.h>
```

```
#include <stdlib.h>
#include <string.h>
#include <dos.h>

#define TRUE    1
#define FALSE   0
#define MAXSTRS 100  /* increase this if you have more env strings */
#define MAXPATH 500  /* max size of path string */
#define PATHSEP ";"  /* separates path names in path */

void main ( int argc, char *argv[ ] )
{
    int i, num, envsize, len, nstrs = 0, found, posi ;
    char option, varstg[MAXPATH], temp[MAXPATH] ;
    char *strptr[MAXSTRS], *lp, far *envp, far *envptr, far *fp, *str ;
    unsigned far *p_psp, far *p_env ;

    struct arenaheader
    {
        char id ;
        unsigned int pid ;
        unsigned int size ;
    } ;
    struct arenaheader far *envah ;

    if ( argc < 2 )
    {
        puts ( "Usage: modipath [ -p newdirname ] [ -a newdirname ]" ) ;
        exit ( 1 ) ;
    }

    /* construct the PSP pointers */
    p_psp = MK_FP ( _psp, 0x16 ) ;  /* pointer to parent's PSP */
    p_env = MK_FP ( *p_psp, 0x2c ) ;  /* pointer to parent's environment
                                          pointer */
    envptr = MK_FP ( *p_env, 0x00 ) ;  /* pointer to parent's environment */
    envah = MK_FP ( *p_env - 1, 0x00 ) ;  /* pointer to parent env MCB */
```

```
envsize = envah->size * 16 ;

/* copy strings from parent's environment ( FAR ) to local strings */
envp = envptr ;

while ( *envp )
{
    fp = envp ;
    len = 0 ;

    while ( *fp )
    {
        len++ ;
        fp++ ;
    }

    strptr[nstrs] = lp = malloc ( len + 1 ) ;

    while ( *envp )
    *lp++ = *envp++ ;

    *lp = '\0' ;
    envp++ ;
    nstrs++ ;
}

/* find the PATH= string among the env vars */
found = FALSE ;

for ( i = 0 ; i < nstrs ; i++ )
{
    if ( strnicmp ( strptr[i], "PATH=", 5 ) == 0 )
    {
        found = TRUE ;
        posi = i ;
        break ;
    }
}
```

```
        }

        if ( found == FALSE )
        {
            printf ( "Can't find path var!\n" ) ;
            exit ( 2 ) ;
        }

        strcpy ( varstg, strptr[i] ) ;

        /* now do what the switches tell us to do */
        for ( i = 1 ; i < argc ; i++ )
        {
            str = argv[i] ;

            if ( *str != '-' )
            {
                printf ( "Begin switches with '-' " ) ;
                exit ( 3 ) ;
            }

            option = tolower ( * ( str + 1 ) ) ;
            i++ ;

            switch ( option )
            {
                case 'a':
                    strcat(varstg, PATHSEP);
                    strcat(varstg, argv[i]);
                    break ;

                case 'p':
                    strcpy ( temp,"PATH=" ) ;
                    strcat ( temp, argv[i] ) ;
                    strcat ( temp, PATHSEP ) ;
                    strcat ( temp, strpbrk ( varstg,"=" ) + 1 ) ;
                    strcpy ( varstg,temp ) ;
```

```
            break ;

        default :
            printf ( "\nImproper choice" ) ;
            exit ( 4 ) ;
    }
}

/* make sure we can copy it all back into the parent's env block */
strptr[posi] = varstg ;
for ( i=0, len=0 ; i < nstrs ; i++ )
    len += strlen ( strptr[i] ) + 1 ;

if ( len + 1 > envsize )
{
    printf ( "\nEnv block too small to store updated PATH string\n" ) ;
    exit ( 5 ) ;
}
else
{
    for ( i = 0 ; i < nstrs ; i++ )
    {
        for ( ; ( *envptr++ = *strptr[i] ++ ) ; )
            ;
        *envptr = '\0' ;
    }
}
```

# 27 *Building Arrays In Expanded Memory*

DOS has a pesky 640 KB memory barrier. When there is a large amount of data, a programmer has to process data separately by reading only part of the data into memory each time. This makes the programming complicated and also degrades the program's performance. To add more memory to the system either Expanded or Extended memory can be installed. Many programs use Extended Memory as if it is Expanded Memory. To achieve this Microsoft provides a memory manager called EMM386.EXE.

In this chapter we would see how to define any array in the Expanded Memory and access the array directly. This way you can handle bigger arrays than what would have been possible using conventional memory.

Expanded memory is the memory beyond DOS's 640 KB limit. The LIM (Lotus-Intel-Microsoft) specification supports up to 32 MB of expanded memory. Because the 8086 family of microprocessors in real mode can physically address only 1 MB of memory, they access expanded memory through a window in their physical address range. Expanded memory is divided into segments called logical pages. These pages are typically of 16 KB size. The computer accesses logical pages through a physical block of memory called a page frame. The page frame contains multiple physical pages, pages that the microprocessor can address directly. Physical pages are also typically 16 KB bytes of memory. This page frame serves as a window into expanded memory. Just as your computer screen is a window into a large spreadsheet, so is the page frame a window into expanded memory.

A logical page of expanded memory can be mapped into any one of the physical pages in the page frame. Thus, a read or write to the physical page actually becomes a read or write to the associated logical page. One logical page can be mapped into the page frame for each physical page. The page frame is located above 640 KB.

The following program shows how all this theory can be put to a practical stint.

```c
#include "dos.h"

#define PAGESIZE 16384

int ems_handle, ems_error, page_frame_address, pages_needed ;
int pages, kilobyte, eachpage, eachelement, elementnum ;

float far *realarray ;

main( )
{
    clrscr( ) ;
    if ( ems_installed( ) == 0 )
```

```
                    {
                        printf ( "\nEMM DOES NOT EXIST " ) ;
                        exit ( 1 ) ;
                    }
                    else
                    {
                        pages = pages_available( ) ;
                        kilobyte = pages * 16 ;
                        printf ( "\nPages in expanded memory = %d", pages ) ;
                        printf ( "\n... That is %d KB", kilobyte ) ;

                        alloc ( pages ) ;

                        if ( ems_error != 0 )
                        {
                            printf ( "\nalloc %d pages error", pages ) ;
                            release( ) ;
                            exit( ) ;
                        }
                        printf ( "\nRead and Write a Real array " ) ;
                        readwrite( ) ;
                        release( ) ;  /* free the memory occupied by the array */
                    }
                }

                ems_installed( )
                {
                    char emm_device_name[9], int_67_device_name[9] ;
                    int p ;
                    char far *p1 ;
                    union REGS i, o ;
                    struct SREGS s ;

                    int_67_device_name[0] = '' ;
                    strcpy ( emm_device_name, "EMMXXXX0" ) ;
```

```
        i.h.ah = 0x35 ;
        i.h.al = 0x67 ;
        intdosx ( &i, &o, &s ) ;
        p1 = MK_FP ( s.es, 10 ) ;

        for( p = 0 ; p <= 7 ; p++ )
        {
            int_67_device_name[p] = *p1 ;
            p1++ ;
        }

        int_67_device_name[p] = 0 ;

        if ( strcmp ( int_67_device_name, emm_device_name ) )
            return ( 0 ) ;
        else
            return ( 1 ) ;
}

pages_available( )
{
        union REGS i, o ;

        i.h.ah = 0x42 ;
        int86 ( 0x67, &i, &o ) ;
        return ( o.x.bx ) ; /* returning pages_available */
}

alloc ( int pages_requested )
{
        union REGS i, o ;

        i.h.ah = 0x41 ;
        int86 ( 0x67, &i, &o ) ;
        page_frame_address = o.x.bx ;
        ems_error = o.h.ah ;
        pages_needed = pages_requested ;
```

```
        i.h.ah = 0x43 ;
        i.x.bx = pages_requested ;
        int86( 0x67, &i, &o ) ;
        ems_handle = o.x.dx ;
        ems_error = o.h.ah ;
}

void mapin ( int logical_page_no, int physical_page_no )
{
        union REGS i, o ;

        i.h.ah = 0x44 ;
        i.x.dx = ems_handle ;
        i.h.al = physical_page_no ;
        i.x.bx = logical_page_no ;
        int86 ( 0x67, &i, &o ) ;

        ems_error = o.h.ah ;
        realarray = MK_FP ( page_frame_address, ( physical_page_no *
                        PAGESIZE ) ) ;
}

release( )
{
        union REGS i, o ;

        i.h.ah = 0x45 ;
        i.x.dx = ems_handle ;
        int86 ( 0x67, &i, &o ) ;

        ems_error = o.h.ah ;
}

readwrite( )
{
        int verifyfail ;
```

```
elementnum = PAGESIZE / sizeof( float ) ;
printf ( "\nSetting up each element of the array..." ) ;

for ( eachpage = 0 ; eachpage < pages ; eachpage++ )
{
    mapin ( eachpage, 0 ) ;
    for ( eachelement = 0 ; eachelement < elementnum ; eachelement++ )
        realarray[ eachelement ] = 3.5 ;
}

printf ( "\nReading back each element of array and verifying...") ;
for ( eachpage = 0 ; eachpage < pages ; eachpage++ )
{
    mapin ( eachpage, 0 ) ;
    for ( eachelement = 0 ; eachelement < elementnum ; eachelement++ )
        verifyfail = realarray[eachelement] != 3.5 ;

    if( verifyfail )
    {
        printf ( "\nverify failed " ) ;
        release( ) ;
        exit( ) ;
    }
}
}
```

By calling the function *emm_installed()* it can be checked whether EMM386.EXE is installed or not. If the function returns TRUE, EMM is installed, otherwise EMM is absent, and you cannot put your data into the Expanded Memory. Of course, if you define many EMS arrays, only a single check for the existence of EMM is necessary.

Next we have determined if there are enough expanded memory pages for our application by calling the function *pages_available()*. This function returns unallocated page numbers (16 KB block). We can allocate memory less than or equal to this value. Next we have called the function *alloc()* to allocate expanded memory pages.

Once the memory is allocated successfully we have mapped a logical page into a physical page by calling the function *mapin()*. If you intend to map more than one logical page into different physical pages, map them in reverse sequence in order to access them continually.

The *readwrite()* function writes the data in expanded memory, just as if it were conventional memory and manages to read it back. Finally, the memory occupied is released when we do not need it any more by calling the function *release()*.

# 28 *Floating Point Formats Not Linked*

Floating Point Formats Not Linked is one of the most common errors that occur while using a majority of C Compilers. Not much, however can be deciphered from this error message. What causes this error to occur? When parsing your source file, if the compiler encounters a reference to the address of a float, it sets a flag to have the linker link in the floating point emulator. A floating point emulator is used to manipulate floating point numbers in runtime library functions like *scanf( )* and *atof( )*. There are some cases in which the reference to the float is a bit obscure and the compiler does not detect the need for the emulator. The most common case is the one which uses *scanf( )* to read a float in an array of structures as shown in the following program.

```
main( )
{
        struct emp
        {
```

```
            char name[20] ;
            int age ;
            float sal ;
        } ;
        struct emp e[5] ;
        int i ;

        clrscr( ) ;
        for ( i = 0 ; i <= 4 ; i++ )
        {
            printf ( "\nEnter name age and salary " ) ;
            scanf ( "%s %d%f",e[i].name, &e[i].age, &e[i].sal ) ;
            printf ( "%s %d %f", e[i].name, e[i].age, e[i].sal ) ;
        }
    }
```

These situations usually occur during the initial stages of program development. Normally, once the program is fully developed, the emulator will be used in such a fashion that the compiler can accurately determine when to link in the emulator.

How can we force the formats to be linked? To force the floating point emulator to be linked into an application, just include the following function in your program:

```
void linkfloat ( void )
{
    float a = 0, *b = &a ;  /* cause emulator to be linked */
    a = *b ;  /* suppress the warning - var not used */
}
```

You do not need to call this function, just include it anywhere in your program. Once your project has reached its full size, you will most likely be able to remove it from the program. The following program shows how to use this function.

```
    main( )
```

```
{
    struct emp
    {
        char name[20] ;
        int age ;
        float sal ;
    } ;
    struct emp e[5] ;
    int i ;

    void linkfloat ( void ) ;
    clrscr( ) ;

    for ( i = 0 ; i <= 4 ; i++ )
    {
        printf ( "\nEnter name age and salary " ) ;
        scanf ( "%s %d %f", e[i].name, &e[i].age, &e[i].sal ) ;
        printf ( "%s %d %f", e[i].name, e[i].age, e[i].sal ) ;
    }
}

void linkfloat ( void )
{
    float a = 0, *b = &a ;  /* cause emulator to be linked */
    a = *b ;  /* suppress warning var not used */
}
```

# 29 *Pointer Errors*

**M**ost of the times beginners in C programming (and at times seasoned programmers) are faced with pointer errors which do not mean much at the first glance. One of the most frequent of these messages is "Null Pointer Assignment". In this chapter I would try to explain the meaning of this error, what causes this error and finally a remedy for it.

The Null Pointer Assignment error is generated only in small and medium memory models. This error occurs in programs which attempt to change the bottom of the data segment.

In Borland's C or C++ compilers, Borland places four zero bytes at the bottom of the data segment, followed by the Borland copyright notice "Borland C++ - Copyright 1991 Borland Intl.". In the small and medium memory models, a null pointer points to DS:0000. Thus assigning a value to the memory referenced by this pointer will overwrite the first zero byte in the data segment. At program termination, the four zeros and the copyright banner are checked. If either has been modified, then the Null Pointer Assignment error is generated. Note that the pointer may not truly be null, but may be a wild pointer that references these key areas in the data segment.

How do we debug a Null Pointer Assignment error? In the Integrated Development Environment set two watches on these key memory locations. These watches, and what they should display in the watch window, are:

```
*(char *)4,42MS     Borland C++ - Copyright 1991 Borland Intl."
(char *)0           00 00 00 00
```

Of course, the copyright banner will vary depending on your version of the Borland C/C++ compiler.

Step through your program using F8 or F7 and monitor these values in the watch window. At the point where one of them changes, you have just executed a statement that uses a pointer that has not been properly initialized.

The most common cause of this error is probably declaring a pointer and then using it before allocating memory for it. For example, compile the following program in the small memory model and execute it:

```c
#include "dos.h"
#include "stdio.h"
#include "string.h"

main( )
{
    char *ptr, *banner ;

    banner = ( char * ) MK_FP ( _DS, 4 ) ;
    printf ( "banner: %s\n", banner ) ;
    strcpy ( ptr, "The world cup saga" ) ;
    printf ( "&ptr = %Fp\n", ( void far* ) &ptr[0] ) ;
    printf ( "banner: %s\n", banner ) ;
}
```

One of the best debugging techniques for catching Null pointer assignment errors is to turn on all warning compiler messages. If the above program is compiled with warnings turned off, no warning messages will be generated. However, if all warnings are turned on, both the *strcpy( )* and *printf( )* calls using the *ptr* variable will generate warnings. You should be particularly suspicious of any warnings that a variable might be used before being initialized, or of a suspicious pointer assignment.

Note that a Null Pointer Assignment error is not generated in all models. In the compact, large and huge memory models, far pointers are used for data. Therefore, a null pointer will reference 0000:0000, or the base of system memory, and using it will not cause a corruption of the key values at the base of the data segment. Modifying the base of system memory usually causes a system crash, however. Although it would be possible that a wild pointer would overwrite the key values, it would not indicate a null pointer. In the tiny memory model, DS = CS = SS. Therefore, using a null pointer will overwrite the beginning of the code segment.

Can anything else generate a Null Pointer Assignment error? Yes, Using a wild pointer that happens to reference the base area of the data segment may cause the same error since this would change the zeros or the copyright banner. Since data corruption or stack corruption could cause an otherwise-valid pointer to be corrupted and point to the base of the data segment, any memory corruption could result in this error being generated. If the pointer used in the program statement which corrupts the key values appears to have been properly initialized, place a watch on that pointer. Step through your program again and watch for its value (address) to change.

# 30 *Getting Input In Graphics Mode*

O ften we are required to receive input in graphics mode. In this chapter I would present a program which demonstrates how to get input from the user in graphics mode, echoed in the current colours and font size and font style. The function responds appropriately to backspace, however no provision is made to guard against overflow of the input buffer or going over the right screen border. The program is given below. The purpose of various functions used in the program is as under:

newline()       Advances the (graphic) text position to the next line.

getgrstring()   Echoes graphically the user input and stores it in a buffer.

cursor()        A helper function for *getgrstring*, to handle the cursor.

```c
#define ON  1
#define OFF 0

#include <graphics.h>
#include <stdio.h>
#include <conio.h>

main( )
{
    char namestring[80], agestring[80] ;
    int age, gd = DETECT, gm ;

    initgraph ( &gd, &gm, "c:\\tc\\bgi" ) ;
    setbkcolor ( BLUE ) ;
    setcolor ( YELLOW ) ;
    settextstyle ( GOTHIC_FONT, HORIZ_DIR, 0 ) ;

    moveto ( 0, 0 ) ;
    outtext ( "Enter your name: " ) ;
    getgrstring ( namestring ) ;
    newline( ) ;

    outtext ( "Enter your age: " ) ;
    getgrstring ( agestring ) ;
    newline( ) ;

    age = atoi ( agestring ) ;
    outtext ( "Name: " ) ;
    outtext ( namestring ) ;
    ++age ;
    sprintf ( agestring, "%d", age ) ;
    newline( ) ;
    outtext ( "Next year, you will be " ) ;
    outtext ( agestring ) ;
    newline( ) ;
    outtext ( "Press key to exit! " ) ;
    getch( ) ;
```

```
        closegraph( ) ;
        restorecrtmode( ) ;
}

newline( )
{
        moveto ( 0, gety( ) + textheight ( "A" ) ) ;
}

getgrstring ( char *inputstring )
{
        int stringindex = 0, oldcolor ;
        char ch, outstring[2] ;

        /* xval will store the screen position for each char */
        int xval[255] ;

        outstring[1] = 0 ;
        xval[0] = getx( ) ;

        do
        {
                cursor ( ON ) ;
                ch = getch( ) ;
                cursor ( OFF ) ;

                if ( ch == 0 )  /* avoid dealing with all special keys */
                        getch( ) ;
                else
                {
                        if ( ch == 8 ) /* backspace */
                        {
                                oldcolor = getcolor( ) ;
                                --stringindex ;

                                if ( stringindex < 0 )
                                        stringindex = 0 ;
```

```
                        /* move to ( old horz position, current vert position ) */
                        moveto ( xval[stringindex], gety( ) ) ;
                        setcolor ( getbkcolor( ) ) ;
                        outstring[0] = inputstring[stringindex] ;
                        outtext ( outstring ) ;
                        moveto ( xval[stringindex], gety( ) ) ;
                        setcolor ( oldcolor ) ;
                }
                else
                {
                        inputstring[stringindex] = ch ;
                        outstring[0] = ch ;
                        outtext ( outstring ) ;
                        ++stringindex ;
                        xval[stringindex] = getx( ) ;
                }
        }
    } while ( ch != 13 && ch != 10 ) ;

    inputstring[stringindex] = 0 ;
}

cursor ( int on )
{
    int curx, oldcolor ;

    /* we'll use an underscore as a cursor */
    char ubarstr[2] = { '_', 0 } ;

    if ( !on )
    {
        oldcolor = getcolor( ) ;
        setcolor ( getbkcolor( ) ) ;
    }

    /* save horizontal position before drawing cursor */
```

```c
    curx = getx ( ) ;
    outtext ( ubarstr ) ;
    moveto ( curx, gety( ) ) ;

    /* if we changed the color to erase cursor, change it back */
    if ( !on )
        setcolor ( oldcolor ) ;
}
```

# 31 *Using Floats in ISRs*

Though rarely, sometimes we may be required to use floating point operations in an interrupt service routine (ISR). In this chapter we would explore how this can be achieved.

The floating point emulator in Turbo C is NOT re-entrant. The 8087 instructions can only be used in interrupt service routines if the chip is present, and all programs with 8087 interrupt handlers are compiled without emulation. Within the interrupt handler, the FNSAVE instruction should be used to save the state of the 8087 chip into a 94-byte state record in memory. After saving the state, an implicit FINIT instruction is executed to bring the co-processor chip into its default state. In this state, exceptions are masked, so divide-by-zeros, overflows, etc. will produce NANs and INFs, not run-time errors. It so happens that this is exactly what we want since a run-time error during an interrupt would completely crash the system. The FNSAVE instruction must be executed before the STI instruction that re-enables interrupts. Furthermore, an FWAIT instruction must precede the STI instruction to make sure that the state has been completely saved. The FRSTOR instruction (it restores the 94-byte co-processor state to the co-processor from the specified memory location) must be followed by an FWAIT to ensure that the state has been completely reloaded before the state variable is removed from the stack. The FWAIT instruction suspends execution of the processor until the co-processor is finished executing.

To achieve all this we can use the standard library function _emit_(). This function allows us to insert literal values directly into the object code as it is compiling. It is used to generate machine language instructions without using inline assembly language. The following program shows how we can obtain sine value of the variable x every time we hit Shift Prtscr. The Shift Prtscr interrupt has been captured for this task using the usual *getvect(), setvect()* functions.

```
#include <stdio.h>
#include <conio.h>
#include <dos.h>
#include <math.h>

void interrupt ( *prev )( ) ;
void interrupt our( ) ;
double x = 0, y = 0 ;

main( )
{
    char ch = 0 ;

    prev = getvect ( 5 ) ; /* the <Shift-PrtScr> interrupt */
    setvect ( 5, our ) ;

    while ( ch != 'q' )
    {
        /* each time you hit Shift-PrtScr x is incremented */
        cprintf ( "%f %f \r\n", x, y ) ;

        if ( kbhit( ) )
            ch = getch( );
```

```
        }
    setvect ( 5, prev ) ;  /* restore original vector for INT 5 */
        }


    void interrupt our( )
        {
        unsigned char state87[94] ;

        __emit__ (
            0xDD,0x76,state87,  /* FNSAVE [BP+<state87] */
            0x9B,  /* FWAIT */
            0xFB   /* STI */
            ) ;

        x += 3.14 / 4 ;
        y = sin ( x ) ;

        __emit__ (
            0x9B,0xDD,0x66,state87,  /* FRSTOR [BP+<state87] */
            0x9B  /* FWAIT */
            ) ;
        }
```

Note that the __emit__() function should be used with extreme
caution. When you use it to place bytes in the instruction code of a
function, if any of these bytes are incorrect the program may mis-
behave and may easily crash your machine.

# 32 *Playing Music*

The speaker in the IBM PC compatibles is made to vibrate by the electrical impulses sent to it by the computer. These vibrations set the air particles around the vibrating source in motion. As the particles bump into one another a sound is produced. We can generate sounds through the speaker by writing a program that turns the speaker on and off by manipulating two speaker bits in the I/O port that provides access to the speaker-control circuitry. When you use this method, your program controls the timing of the pulse and the resulting sound frequency. As with most other parts of the PC, the speaker is manipulated by sending certain values to a specific port. The speaker is controlled by changing the values of bits 0 and 1 at I/O port 97. Only 2 of the port's 8 bits are used by the speaker: the low-order bits numbered 0 and 1. The other 6 bits are used for other purposes, so it is important that you don't disturb them while working with the speaker.

The lowest bit, bit 0, controls transmission of the timer chip's output signal to the speaker. The second bit, bit 1, controls the pulsing of the speaker. Both bits must be set to make the speaker respond to the timer chip's signal.

The following program plays the notes in an octave on the speaker. Not being a musician I fear it may lack a great deal. However, you would get an idea of how to play notes. I would be very grateful to see (and hear) some improvements, so please let me know what you come up with.

```
#include <dos.h>

#define C  0
#define Df 1
#define D  2
#define Ef 3
#define E  4
#define F  5
#define Fs 6
#define G  7
#define Af 8
#define A  9
#define Bf 10
#define B  11


#define REPEAT 12  /* repeat from beginning */
#define SO 13  /* switch octaves */
#define R 14  /* rest (duration follows) */
#define END 15  /* end of the tune */

/* durations */
#define L1  1
#define L2  2
#define L4  4
#define L8  8
#define L16 16
#define L32 32
#define L64 64
```

```
float notes[7][12] =
{
        {
                130.81, 138.59, 146.83, 155.56, 164.81, 174.61, 185.0,
                196.0, 207.65, 220.0, 227.31, 246.96
        },
        {
                261.63, 277.18, 293.66, 311.13, 329.63, 349.23, 369.99,
                392.0, 415.3, 440.0, 454.62, 493.92
        },
        {
                523.25, 554.37, 587.33, 622.25, 659.26, 698.46, 739.99,
                783.99, 830.61, 880.0, 909.24, 987.84
        },
        {
                1046.5, 1108.73, 1174.66, 1244.51, 1328.51, 1396.91,
                1479.98, 1567.98, 1661.22, 1760.0, 1818.48, 1975.68
        },
        {
                2093.0, 2217.46, 2349.32, 2489.02, 2637.02, 2793.83,
                2959.96, 3135.96, 3322.44, 3520.0, 3636.96, 3951.36
        },
        {
                4186.0, 4434.92, 4698.64, 4978.04, 5274.04, 5587.66,
                5919.92, 6271.92, 6644.88, 7040.0, 7273.92, 7902.72
        },
        {
                8372.0, 8869.89, 9397.28, 9956.08, 10548.08, 11175.32, 11839.84,
                12543.84,13289.76, 14080.0, 14547.84, 15805.44
        }
};

char tune[ ] = {
                SO,3,C,L8,D,L8,E,L8,F,L8,G,L8,A,L8,B,L8,SO,4,C,L8,R,L4,
                SO,4,C,L8,SO,3,B,L8,A,L8,G,L8,F,L8,E,L8,D,L8,C,L8,
                END
        };
```

```
char note, duration, octave, *ptr, *start, sp_on, sp_off ;

union
{
    long count ;
    unsigned char byte[2] ;
} p ;

main( )
{
    start = ptr = tune ;
    sp_off = inportb ( 97 ) ;
    sp_on = sp_off | 3 ;
    duration = 0 ;
    playtune( ) ;
}


playtune( )
{
    while ( 1 )
    {
        if ( duration )
        {
            delay ( 500 ) ;
            duration-- ;
        }
        else
        {
            note = *ptr ;
            switch ( note )
            {
                case 12:
                    ptr = start ;
                    break ;
                case 13:
```

```
            ptr++ ;
            octave = *ptr ;
            ptr++ ;
            break ;

    case 14:
            ptr++ ;
            duration = *ptr ;
            outportb ( 97, sp_off ) ;
            ptr++ ;
            break ;

    case 15:
            outportb ( 97, sp_off ) ;
            return ;

    default:
            ptr++ ;
            duration = *ptr ;
            p.count = 1193280 / notes[octave][note] ;
            outportb ( 67, 182 ) ;
            outportb ( 66, p.byte[0] ) ;
            outportb ( 66, p.byte[1] ) ;
            outportb ( 97, sp_on ) ;
            ptr++ ;
        }
    }
}
}
```

# 33 *Music In*

## *Background*

IN the last chapter we saw how to play notes in an octave by controlling their frequency as well as the duration. However, when the notes were being played nothing else was being done. This time I am presenting a program which plays the tune in the background while a message is being printed in the foreground. Here is the program to achieve this...

```
#include <dos.h>

/* the note defines */
#define C  0
#define Cs 1
#define Db 1
#define D  2
#define Ds 3
#define Eb 3
#define E  4
#define F  5
#define Fs 6
#define Gb 6
```

```
#define G  7
#define Gs 8
#define Ab 8
#define A  9
#define As 10
#define Bb 10
#define B  11

/* pseudo operations defines */
#define REPEAT 12 /* repeat from beginning */
#define SO 13 /* switch octaves  */
#define R 14 /* rest ( duration follows ) */
#define END 15 /* end of the song  */

/* duration defines */
#define L1  1
#define L2  2
#define L4  4
#define L8  8
#define L16 16
#define L32 32

float notes[7][12] =
{
    {
        130.81, 138.59, 146.83, 155.56, 164.81, 174.61, 185.0,
        196.0, 207.65, 220.0, 227.31, 246.96
    },
    {
        261.63, 277.18, 293.66, 311.13, 329.63, 349.23, 369.99,
        392.0, 415.3, 440.0, 454.62, 493.92
    },
    {
        523.25, 554.37, 587.33, 622.25, 659.26, 698.46, 739.99,
        783.99, 830.61, 880.0, 909.24, 987.84
    },
    {
```

```
                1046.5, 1108.73, 1174.66, 1244.51, 1328.51, 1396.91,
                1479.98, 1567.98, 1661.22, 1760.0, 1818.48, 1975.68
        },
        {
                2093.0, 2217.46, 2349.32, 2489.02, 2637.02, 2793.83,
                2959.96, 3135.96, 3322.44, 3520.0, 3636.96, 3951.36
        },
        {
                4186.0, 4434.92, 4698.64, 4978.04, 5274.04, 5587.66,
                5919.92, 6271.92, 6644.88, 7040.0, 7273.92, 7902.72
        },
        {
                8372.0, 8869.89, 9397.28, 9956.08, 10548.08, 11175.32, 11839.84,
                12543.84,13289.76, 14080.0, 14547.84, 15805.44
        }
};
char tune[ ] = {
                SO,3,C,L8,D,L8,E,L8,F,L8,G,L8,A,L8,B,L8,SO,4,C,
                L8,R,L4,REPEAT
                };
char note, duration, octave, *ptr, *start, sp_on, sp_off ;

union
{
    long count ;
    unsigned char byte[2] ;
} p ;


void install( ), restore( ) ;
void interrupt our( ) ;
void interrupt ( *prev )( ) ;

main( )
{
    start = ptr = tune ;
```

```
        install( ) ;

        while ( !kbhit( ) )
            printf ( "\nPlaying a tune in the background" ) ;

        restore( ) ;
}

void install( )
{
        sp_off = inportb ( 97 ) ;
        sp_on = sp_off I 3 ;
        duration = 0 ;
        prev = getvect ( 0x1c ) ;
        disable( ) ;
        setvect ( 0x1c, &our ) ;
        enable( ) ;
}

void restore( )
{
        /* restores the old timer vector and speaker state */
        disable( ) ;
        setvect ( 0x1c, prev ) ;
        enable( ) ;
        outportb ( 97, sp_off ) ;
}

void interrupt our( )
{
        if ( duration )
            duration-- ;
        else
        {
            note = *ptr ;
            switch ( note )
            {
```

```
            case 12:
                ptr = start ;
                break ;

            case 13:
                ptr++ ;
                octave = *ptr ;
                ptr++ ;
                break ;

            case 14:
                ptr++ ;
                duration = *ptr ;
                outportb ( 97, sp_off ) ;
                ptr++ ;
                break ;

            case 15:
                break ;

            default:
                ptr++ ;
                duration = *ptr ;
                p.count = 1193280 / notes[octave][note] ;
                outportb ( 67, 182 ) ;
                outportb ( 66, p.byte[0] ) ;
                outportb ( 66, p.byte[1] ) ;
                outportb ( 97, sp_on ) ;
                ptr++ ;
                break ;
        }
    }
}
```

# 34 *Printing Graphics*

**W**hen you send a character to the printer, it prints the character using a pattern of dots stored in memory. However, if we are to print some graphics on the printer the pattern of dots are not known to it. In such cases one needs to control the individual dots that are printed. To achieve this we need to understand how the print head works. The print head consists of nine pins stacked one above the other. The print head can therefore print a column upto nine dots at a time. As the print head moves across the paper it strikes the appropriate pins against the ribbon forming columns of dots on each line. To print graphics we need to tell the printer two things:

(a)  Which pins to print in each column.
(b)  How many columns there will be in a line.

To tell the printer which pins to print in each column, you need a way to identify the pins in the print head. There are numbers associated with each pin. If the pins are numbered from 1 to 9 from top to bottom then the numbers associated with them are 1, 2, 4, 8, 16, etc. We can print any combination of pins by sending to the printer the sum of pin numbers we want to print. For example, to print first three pins from the top we need to send a value 7 (1+2+4) to the printer.

With this much theoretical background let us write a program which will print the graphics drawn on the screen onto the printer.

```c
#include <graphics.h>
#include <stdio.h>
#include <io.h>

#define ESC  27
#define LPT1 0
#define LPT2 1
#define write_to_prn( x )  biosprint ( 0, x, LPT1 )

main( )
{
    int gd = DETECT, gm, x, y ;

    initgraph ( &gd, &gm, "c:\\tc\\bgi" ) ;

    x = getmaxx( ) ;
    y = getmaxy( ) ;
    rectangle ( 0, 0, x, y ) ;
    circle ( 300, 200, 100 ) ;
    circle ( 300, 200, 50 ) ;
    circle ( 300, 200, 30 ) ;
    line ( 200, 350, 400, 350 ) ;
    line ( 250, 360, 350, 360 ) ;
    line ( 275, 370, 325, 370 ) ;

    printimage ( 0, 0, x, y ) ;  /* print the entire screen */

    closegraph( ) ;
}

/* graphics print function */
```

```
printimage ( int x1, int y1, int x2, int y2 )
{
    int x, y, width ;

    width = x2 - x1 ;

    /* initialize line spacing to 7/72" */
    write_to_prn ( ESC ) ;
    write_to_prn ( '1' ) ;

    for ( y = y1 ; y < y2 ; y += 8 )
    {
        set_bit_image_mode ( width ) ;

        for ( x = x1 ; x < x2 ; x++ )
            write_to_prn ( getpins ( x, y ) ) ;

        write_to_prn ( '\n' ) ;
    }
}

/* sets Epson printer to bit image mode */
set_bit_image_mode ( int num )
{
    int n1, n2 ;

    /* num is the number of bytes to print */
    n1 = num % 256 ;
    n2 = num / 256 ;
    write_to_prn ( ESC ) ;
    write_to_prn ( '*' ) ;
    write_to_prn ( 4 ) ;
    write_to_prn ( n1 ) ;
    write_to_prn ( n2 ) ;
}

/* get pixels from screen & convert them to the printer's pin order */
```

```
getpins ( int x, int y )
{
    unsigned char pins ;
    pins = ( getpixel ( x, y++ ) == 0 ) ? 0 : 128 ;
    pins |= ( getpixel ( x, y++ ) == 0 ) ? 0 : 64 ;
    pins |= ( getpixel ( x, y++ ) == 0 ) ? 0 : 32 ;
    pins |= ( getpixel ( x, y++ ) == 0 ) ? 0 : 16 ;
    pins |= ( getpixel ( x, y++ ) == 0 ) ? 0 : 8 ;
    pins |= ( getpixel ( x, y++ ) == 0 ) ? 0 : 4 ;
    pins |= ( getpixel ( x, y++ ) == 0 ) ? 0 : 2 ;
    pins |= ( getpixel ( x, y ) == 0 ) ? 0 : 1 ;
    return pins ;
}
```

# 35 _Trapping Disk Errors_

In this chapter we would explore how to establish a hardware error handler. Turbo C provides a standard library function called _harderr()_ for this purpose. It establishes a hardware errorhandler for the current program. This error handler is invoked whenever an interrupt 0x24 occurs. The function pointed to by handler will be called when such an interrupt occurs. The handler function will be called with the following arguments:

handler ( int errval, int ax, int bp, int si ) ;

where, _errval_ is the error code set in the DI register by DOS. _ax_, _bp_, and _si_ are the values DOS sets for the AX, BP, and SI registers, respectively. The value of _ax_ indicates whether a disk error or other device error was encountered. If ax is non-negative, a disk error was encountered; otherwise, the error was a device error. For a disk error, _ax_ ANDed with _0x00FF_ will give the failing drive number. _bp_ and _si_ together point to the device driver header of the failing driver, _bp_ contains the segment address, and _si_ the offset. The function pointed to by handler is not called directly. _harderr()_ establishes a DOS interrupt handler that calls the function. The handler must return 0

for ignore, 1 for retry, and 2 for abort. The following program shows
how this can be achieved.

```
#include <stdio.h>
#include <conio.h>
#include <dos.h>

#define IGNORE 0
#define RETRY  1
#define ABORT  2

int buf[500] ;

/* error messages for trapping disk problems */
char *err_msg[ ] = {
                "Write protect", "Unknown unit",
                "Drive not ready", "Unknown command",
                "Data error ( CRC )", "Bad request",
                "Seek error", "Unknown media type",
                "Sector not found", "Printer out of paper",
                "Write fault", "Read fault", "General failure",
                "Reserved", "Reserved", "Invalid disk change"
                                } ;
int handler ( int errval, int ax, int bp, int si ) ;

main( )
{
        harderr ( handler ) ;
        clrscr( ) ;
        printf ( "Make sure there is no disk in drive A:\n" ) ;
        printf ( "Press any key ....\n" ) ;
        getch( ) ;
        printf ( "Trying to access drive A:\n" ) ;
        fopen ( "A:temp.dat", "w" ) ;
}

/* user error interface */
```

```
error_win ( char *msg )
{
    int retval ;
    cputs ( msg ) ;

    /* prompt for user to press a key to abort, retry, ignore */
    while ( 1 )
    {
        retval= getch( ) ;
        if ( retval == 'a' || retval == 'A' )
        {
            retval = ABORT ;
            break ;
        }

        if ( retval == 'r' || retval == 'R' )
        {
            retval = RETRY ;
            break ;
        }

        if ( retval == 'i' || retval == 'I' )
        {
            retval = IGNORE ;
            break ;
        }
    }
    return ( retval ) ;
}

int handler ( int errval, int ax, int bp, int si )
{
    static char msg[80] ;
    unsigned di ;
    int drive, errorno ;

    di = _DI ;
```

```
/* if this is not a disk error */
if ( ax < 0 )
{
    error_win ( "Device error" ) ; /* report the error */

    /* return to the program directly requesting abort */
    hardretn ( ABORT ) ;
}

drive = ax & 0x00FF ;
errorno = di & 0x00FF ;
/* report which error it was */
sprintf ( msg, "\r\nError: %s on drive %c:-- Abort, Retry, Ignore: ",
err_msg[errorno], 'A' + drive ) ;

/* return to the program via dos interrupt 0x23 with abort,
retry or ignore as input by the user */
hardresume ( error_win ( msg ) ) ;

    return ABORT ;
}
```

# 36 *Implementing Complex Numbers*

How do we implement complex numbers in C? It is quite straightforward to implement complex numbers and the functions to manipulate them if you know how to use structures. The following program shows the implementation in its simplest forms.

```
# include "stdio.h"
typedef struct
{
    double real ;
    double imag ;
} complex ;

void main( )
{
    complex complex_set ( double, double ) ;
    complex complex_add ( complex, complex ) ;
```

```
        complex complex_mul ( complex, complex ) ;
        void complex_print ( complex c ) ;
        complex a, b, c, d ;

        a = complex_set ( 1.0, 1.0 ) ;
        b = complex_set ( 2.0, 2.0 ) ;
        c = complex_add ( a, b ) ;
        d = complex_mul ( a, b ) ;
        printf ( "\nc = " ) ;
        complex_print ( c ) ;
        printf ( "\nd = " ) ;
        complex_print ( d ) ;
}

complex complex_set ( double r, double i )
{
    complex temp ;
    temp.real = r ;
    temp.imag = i ;
    return temp ;
}

void complex_print ( complex t )
{
    printf ( "(%g, %g)", t.real, t.imag ) ;
}

complex complex_add ( complex c1, complex c2 )
{
    complex temp ;
    temp.real = c1.real + c2.real ;
    temp.imag = c1.imag + c2.imag ;
    return temp ;
}

complex complex_mul ( complex c1, complex c2 )
{
```

```
        complex temp ;
        temp.real = c1.real * c2.real - c1.imag * c2.imag ;
        temp.imag = c1.real * c2.imag + c2.real * c1.imag ;
        return temp ;
}
```

The program is quite simple to understand. As we know, a complex number consists of a real part and an imaginary part. Hence to handle them we have built a structure. Note that the *%g* format used in the function *complex_print( )* prints the resulting complex number's real and imaginary part either in fractional or exponential form based on the value and precision of the real and complex parts. Also, since the functions *complex_set( )*, *complex_add( )* and *complex_mul( )* return values of the type *complex* their prototypes are so defined. Instead of adding two complex numbers by calling the function *complex_add( )* C++ offers a more intuitive method for performing addition through a facility called overloaded + operator.

# 37

# *EXE2BIN*
# *Utility*

The popular EXE2BIN utility available with DOS converts the executable files to the binary format (a memory image of the program). In this chapter we would develop a parallel utility whose usage is same as EXE2BIN except:

- The output file produced has a .COM extension rather than .BIN
- The binary fixup option is not supported
- The checksum is not verified

Here is the program...

```
#include "stdio.h"
#include "dos.h"
#include "stdlib.h"

/* error codes */
#define BADSIGN  1
#define HASRELO  2
#define HAS_SS  3
#define HAS_CS  4
```

```
#define BAD_IP  5
#define TOO_BIG  6

/* EXE file header */
struct header
{
    char id[2] ;              /* EXE file signature: "MZ" */
    unsigned last_page,       /* image size mod 512 (valid bytes in last page) */
    pages,                    /* number of 512-byte pages in image */
    num_reloc,                /* Count of relocation table entries */
    hdr_size,                 /* size of header, in paragraphs */
    min_para,                 /* min required memory (in paragraphs) */
    max_para,                 /* max required memory (in paragraphs) */
    ss,                       /* stack seg offset in load module */
    sp,                       /* initial value of SP. */
    checksum,                 /* file checksum */
    ip,                       /* initial value of IP */
    cs,                       /* CS offset in load module */
    relo_start,               /* offset of first relo item */
    overlaynum ;              /* overlay number */
} h ;

FILE *fs, *ft ; /* input and output file streams */

char source[67], target[67] ;     /* input and output file names */
unsigned long code_start,         /* offset of program image in EXE file */
              code_size;          /* size of program image, in bytes */

main ( int argc, char *argv[ ] )
{
    char *ptr ;

    if ( argc < 2 || argc > 3 )
    {
        printf ( "usage: exe2com  file  [file]\n" ) ;
        exit ( 1 ) ;
    }
```

```
/* if input file has no extension, add .EXE */
strcpy ( source, strlwr ( argv[1] ) ) ;
if ( strchr ( source, '.' ) == NULL )
    strcat ( source, ".exe" ) ;

/* get or construct output file name */
if ( argc == 3 )
    strcpy ( target, strlwr ( argv[2] ) ) ;
else
    strcpy ( target, source ) ;

/* check output extension - change EXE to COM, or add COM */
if ( ( ( ptr = strchr ( target, '.' ) ) == NULL )
    strcat ( target, ".com" ) ;
else
{
    if ( strcmp ( ptr, ".exe" ) == 0 )
        strcpy ( ptr, ".com" ) ;
}

/* open input and output files */
if ( ( fs = fopen ( source, "rb" ) ) == NULL )
{
    printf ( "\nUnable to open input file %s", source ) ;
    exit ( 1 ) ;
}

if ( ( ft = fopen ( target, "wb" ) ) == NULL )
{
    printf ( "\nUnable to open target file %s", target ) ;
    exit ( 1 ) ;
}

readheader( ) ;
convert( ) ;
}
```

The program begins with a structure that defines the header present at the beginning of any .EXE file. The comments should help you understand its various components. The program then interprets the command line arguments and constructs the input and output filenames with .EXE and .COM extensions respectively. Then it opens the two files and calls the functions *readheader()* and *convert()*. These are the most crucial functions in this program. Before looking into these functions let first find out the constraints under which the conversion from .EXE to .COM is possible. These are:

- The first two bytes in the EXE file header must be 'M' and 'Z'.
- There should be no relocatable items.
- There should be no stack segment.
- The code and data portions of the file combined must not exceed 64 KB.
- Initial value of IP in the header should be either 0 or 100.

The program calls the function *readheader()* and checks whether the above constraints are met. If the program fails to meet these conditions then a function *exit_on_error()* is called which flashes the appropriate message and exits. If the conversion is possible then the function *convert()* is called which reads the image (which follows the header), and dumps it into the output file. To carry this out properly the program image's offset and the program size are calculated.

The program size is given by:

```
        512 * ( number of EXE pages - 1 )
    +   valid bytes in last EXE page
    -   offset of program image in EXE file
```

While converting if IP is nonzero, the program skips the first IP bytes of the program image, and copies IP bytes fewer than the actual size.

```
/* read and check the EXE file header */
readheader( )
{
```

```
        /* read the formatted portion of the header */
        fread ( &h, sizeof ( struct header ), 1, fs ) ;

        /* check whether the file is convertible */

        if ( strncmp (h.id, "MZ", 2 ) )
            exit_on_error ( BADSIGN ) ;
        if ( h.num_reloc)
            exit_on_error ( HASRELO ) ;
        if ( h.ss || h.sp)
            exit_on_error ( HAS_SS ) ;
        if ( h.ip != 0 && h.ip != 0x100 )
            exit_on_error ( BAD_IP ) ;

        /* compute offset of program image and program size */
        code_start = ( ( unsigned long ) h.hdr_size) << 4 ;
        code_size = ( unsigned long ) ( h.pages - 1 ) * 512
                    + ( h.last_page ? h.last_page : 512 )
                    - code_start ;

        if ( code_size >= 65536L )
            exit_on_error ( TOO_BIG ) ;

        /* warn if COM file and IP != 0x100 */
        if ( strcmp ( strchr ( target, '.' ), ".com" ) == 0 && h.ip != 0x100 )
            printf ( "\nWarning: COM file, initial IP not 100H" ) ;
}

/* read the image (which follows the header), and output it to disk */
convert( )
{
        char buffer[ 512 ];
        unsigned wsize;

        /* seek to start of program image, skipping IP bytes */
        fseek ( fs, code_start + h.ip, 0 ) ;
```

```
/* reduce the "remaining" byte count by IP bytes */
code_size -= h.ip ;

/* read blocks and copy to output */
while ( code_size )
{
    /* read block */
    fread ( buffer, 1, 512, fs ) ;

    /* set count of bytes to write, write block */
    wsize = ( unsigned ) ( code_size > 512 ? 512 : code_size ) ;
    fwrite ( buffer, wsize, 1, ft ) ;

    /* subtract bytes written from remaining byte count */
    code_size -= wsize ;
}

/* all done, close the two files */
fclose ( fs ) ;
fclose ( ft ) ;
}

/* display an error message, delete output file, and exit */
exit_on_error ( int num )
{
    char str[80] ;

    switch ( num )
    {
        case BADSIGN :
                        strcpy ( str, "invalid EXE file signature" ) ;
                        break;

        case HASRELO :
                        strcpy ( str, "EXE has relocatable items" ) ·
                        break;
```

```
                case HAS_SS :
                            strcpy ( str, "EXE has stack segment" ) ;
                            break;

                case HAS_CS :
                            strcpy ( str, "EXE has nonzero CS" ) ;
                            break;

                case BAD_IP :
                            strcpy ( str, "IP not 0 or 100H" ) ;
                            break;

                case TOO_BIG :
                            strcpy ( str, "Program exceeds 64 KB" ) ;
                            break;

                default:
                            strcpy ( str, "Unknown error" ) ;
        }

        printf ( "%s, can't convert\n", str ) ;

        fclose ( fs ) ;
        fclose ( ft ) ;
        unlink ( target ) ;
        exit ( 1 ) ;
}
```

# 38

# *Variably*
# *Dimensioned*
# *Arrays*

hile dealing with Scientific or Engineering problems one
is often required to make use of multi-dimensioned array.
However, when it comes to passing multi-dimensional
arrays to a function C is found wanting. This is because the C
compiler wants to know the size of all but the first dimension of any
array passed to a function. For instance, we can define a function
*compute ( int n, float x[ ])*, but not *compute (int n, x[ ] [ ])*.

Thus, C can deal with variably dimensioned 1-D arrays, but when an
array has more than one dimension, the C compiler has to know the
size of all dimensions except the first expressed as a constant. This
problem has long been recognized, and some of the solutions that are
often used are:

(a)    Declare the arrays in the functions to be big enough to tackle
       all possible situations. This can lead to a wastage of lot of
       precious memory in most cases.

(b)    Another solution is to construct multiple-dimension array as
       an array of pointers. For example, a matrix (2-D array) of floats
       can be declared as a 1-D array of float pointers, with each
       element pointing to an array of floats. The problem with this
       method is that the calling function has to define all arrays in
       this fashion. This means that any other computations done on
       the arrays must take this special structure into account.

Another easy solution, though seldom used, exists. This is based on
the following method:

-    Pass the array to the function as though it is a pointer to
     an array of floats (or the appropriate data type), no matter
     how many dimensions the array actually has, along with
     the dimensions of the array.
-    Reference individual array elements as offsets from this
     pointer.
-    Write your algorithm so that array elements are accessed
     in storage order.

The following program for multiplying two matrices illustrates this
procedure.

```
# define M 3
# define N 2
# define P 4

float a[M][N], b[N][P], c[M][P] ;
void mulmat ( int, int, int, float *, float *, float * ) ;

main( )
{
    int i, j ;

    for ( i = 0 ; i < M ; i++ )
    {
        for ( j = 0 ; j < N ; j++ )
```

```
                a[i][j] = i + j ;
        }

        for ( i = 0 ; i < N ; i++ )
        {
            for( j = 0 ; j < P ; j++ )
                b[i][j] = i + j ;
        }

        mulmat ( M, N, P, a, b, c ) ;

        for ( i = 0 ; i < M ; i++ )
        {
            printf ( "\n" ) ;
            for ( j = 0 ; j < P ; j++ )
                printf ( "%f\t", c[i][j] ) ;
        }
    }

void mulmat ( int m, int n, int p, float *a, float *b, float *c )
    {
        float *ptrtob, *ptrtoc ;
        int i, j, k, nc ;

        /* set all elements of matrix c to 0 */
        for ( i = 0 ; i < m * p ; i++ )
            *( c + i ) = 0 ;

        for ( i = 0 ; i < m ; i++ )
        {
            ptrtob = b ;
            for ( k = 0 ; k < n ; k++ )
            {
                ptrtoc = c ;

                for ( j = 0 ; j < p ; j++ )
                    *ptrtoc++ += *a * *ptrtob++ ;
```

```
            a++ ;
        }
        c += p ;
    }
}
```

We know that C stores array elements in a row-major order. Hence
to ensure that the elements are accessed in the storage order the above
program uses a variation of the normal matrix- multiplication procedure. The pseudocode for this is given below:

```
for i = 1 to m
    for j = 1 to p
        c[i][j] = 0
    end
    for k = 1 to n
        for j = 1 to p
            c[i][j] = c[i][j] + a[i][k] * b[k][j]
        end
    end
end
```

This idea can be extended in a straightforward manner to array with
more than two dimensions. Try to.

# *39* *Calculating Wasted Bytes On Disk*

W hen a file gets stored on the disk, at a time DOS allocates one cluster for it. A cluster is nothing but a group of sectors. However, since all file sizes cannot be expected to be a multiple of 512 bytes, when a file gets stored often part of the cluster remains unoccupied. This space goes waste unless the file size grows to occupy these wasted bytes. The following program finds out how much space is wasted for all files in all the directories of the current drive.

```
#include <dir.h>
#include <dos.h>
#include <stdio.h>
#include <string.h>
#include <stdlib.h>

unsigned bytes_per_cluster ;
unsigned long wasted_bytes ;
```

```
unsigned long num_files = 0 ;

main( )
{
    int ptr = 0, flag = 0, first = 0 ;
    struct ffblk f[50] ;
    struct dfree free ;

    /* get cluster information and calculate bytes per cluster */
    getdfree ( 0, &free ) ;
    bytes_per_cluster = free.df_bsec * free.df_sclus ;

    chdir ( "\\" ) ;

    /* check out files in root directory first */
    cal_waste( ) ;

    /* loop until all directories scanned */
    while ( ptr != -1 )
    {
        /* should I do a findfirst or a findnext? */
        if ( first == 0 )
                flag = findfirst ( "*.*", &f[ptr], FA_DIREC ) ;
        else
                flag = findnext ( &f[ptr] ) ;

        while ( flag == 0 )
        {
            /* make sure its a directory and skip over . & .. entries */
            if ( f[ptr].ff_attrib == FA_DIREC && f[ptr].ff_name[0] != '.' )
            {
                flag = chdir ( f[ptr].ff_name ) ; /* try changing directories */
                if ( flag == 0 )  /* did change dir work? */
                {
                    cal_waste( ) ;
                    first = 0 ;  /* set for findfirst on next pass */
                    break ;
```

```
                }
            }
        flag = findnext ( &f[ptr] ) ;  /* search for more dirs */
    }

    if ( flag != 0 || ptr == 49 )  /* didn't find any more dirs */
    {
        ptr-- ;
        chdir ( ".." ) ;  /* go back one level */
        first = 1 ;  /* set to findnext on next pass */
    }
    else
        ptr++ ;
    }
    printf ( "\nThere are %lu bytes wasted in %lu files.\n", wasted_bytes,
            num_files ) ;
}

cal_waste( )
{
    int flag = 0 ;
    long full_cluster ;
    struct ffblk ff ;

    /* look for all file types */
    flag = findfirst ( "*.*", &ff, FA_RDONLY | FA_HIDDEN | FA_SYSTEM |
                    FA_ARCH ) ;
    while ( flag == 0 )
    {
        num_files++ ;
        full_cluster = ff.ff_fsize / bytes_per_cluster * bytes_per_cluster ;
        wasted_bytes += bytes_per_cluster - ( ff.ff_fsize - full_cluster ) ;
        flag = findnext ( &ff ) ;
    }
}
```

# 40 *Function Documentor*

Often C programs contain numerous functions. In such cases, to maintain the programs it is important to maintain a list of functions present in the program along with their parameters and return types. It makes sense in automating this process rather than maintaining the list manually. The following program searches a C source files and displays a sorted list of all function definitions in it along with the function return type, line number in which the function is defined and the name of the file in which the definition appears.

```
#include <stdio.h>
#include <ctype.h>
#include <stdlib.h>
#include <string.h>

#define NAMESIZE 13  /* size of filename */
#define MAXSTR   50  /* max length of function name */
#define MAXLINE  21  /* max screen lines */
#define MAX      100 /* max functions in a file */

char *typearray[ ] = { "FILE", "char", "double", "float", "int", "long",
```

```
                            "static", "struct", "unsigned", "void" } ;
int  entry ;
FILE *fp ;

struct record
{
    char name[MAXSTR] ;  /* name of function */
    char type[NAMESIZE] ;  /* type of function */
    char file[NAMESIZE] ;  /* name of C source file */
    unsigned int line ;  /* line number of function definition */
} table[MAX] ;

int main ( int argc, char *argv[ ] )
{
    int qs_compare( ) ;

    if ( argc != 2 )
    {
        printf ( "Usage: findfunc filename" ) ;
        exit ( 1 ) ;
    }

    if ( ( ( fp = fopen ( argv[1], "r" ) ) == NULL )
    {
        printf ( "\nUnable to open file" ) ;
        exit ( 2 ) ;
    }

    read_file ( argv[1] ) ;
    qsort ( table, entry, sizeof ( struct record ), qs_compare ) ;
    display_results( ) ;  /* show sorted results */
}

int qs_compare ( char *s1, char *s2 )
{
    return ( strcmp ( s1, s2 ) ) ;
}
```

```c
display_results( )
{
    int row = 0, i ;
    clrscr( );

    for ( i = 0 ; i < entry ; i++ )
    {
        printf ( "\n%-50s  %-8s %4d %s",
                table[i].name, table[i].type, table[i].line, table[i].file ) ;

        row++ ;
        if ( row > MAXLINE )
        {
            printf ( "\nPress any key to continue..." ) ;
            getch( ) ;
            clrscr( ) ;
            row = 0 ;
        }
    }
}

read_file ( char *fname )
{
    char *bptr, buff[300], buff1[300], buff2[300], *c, *decl, *sptr, *p,
        temp[50], *ptr ;
    int bs_compare( ) ;
    int lines, nel, wide, len ;

    wide = sizeof ( typearray[0] ) ;
    nel  = sizeof ( typearray ) / wide ;
    lines = 0 ;

    while ( fgets ( buff, 250, fp ) != NULL )
    {
        lines++ ;
```

```
/* remove white space at beginning of line */
ptr = ltrim ( buff ) ;

strcpy ( buff1, ptr ) ;
strcpy ( buff2, buff1 ) ;

sptr = strchr ( buff2, '(' ) ;  /* look for opening parentheses */

if ( sptr == NULL )  /* no parentheses, keep reading */
    continue ;

sptr = strtok ( buff1, " " ) ;  /* look for spaces */

if ( sptr == NULL )
    continue ;

/* token found, find out whether it is in the type specifier list */
bptr = bsearch ( &sptr, typearray, nel, wide, bs_compare ) ;

/* if absent */
if ( bptr == NULL )
    continue ;

/* check whether the statement is assignment statement */
p = strstr ( buff2, sptr ) ;
p = p + strlen ( sptr ) + 1 ;

while ( isalpha ( *p ) || *p == '_' || isdigit ( *p ) || isspace ( *p ) )
    p++ ;

if ( *p == '=' )
    continue ;
else
{
    len = strlen ( buff2 ) ;
    if ( len > MAXSTR )
        len = MAXSTR - 1 ;  /* chop the string if too long */
```

```
            else
                    len-- ;  /* get rid of newline if too short */
        }

        buff2[len] = '\0' ;  /* and make it a string */

        /* get a pointer to space between type specifier and name */
        decl = c = strchr ( buff2, ' ' ) ;
        while ( *decl == ' ' || *decl == '\t' )
            decl++ ;

        /* copy the function info. to table */
        strcpy ( table[entry].name, decl ) ;
        strncpy ( table[entry].type, buff2, c - buff2 ) ;
        strcpy ( table[entry].file, fname ) ;
        table[entry].line = lines ;

        entry++ ;
        if ( entry > MAX )
        {
            clrscr( ) ;
            printf ( "Out of memory" ) ;
            exit ( 2 ) ;
        }
    }
}

int bs_compare ( char **s1, char **s2 )
{
    return ( strcmp ( *s1, *s2 ) ) ;
}

ltrim ( char *s, char *t )
{
    while ( *s == ' ' || *s == '\t' || *s == '\n' )
            s++ ;
```

```
        return ( s ) ;
   }
```

The program receives the filename in which the functions are to be searched as a command line argument. Once the file has been opened the *read_file()* function searches for the function definitions in this file and having located them stores their information in the array of structures *table[ ]* . Once the entire file has been scanned for the function definitions the information in the array *table[ ]* is sorted using the standard library function *qsort()*. The sorted results are displayed on the screen using the function *display_results()*.

The *read_file()* function is the most important function in this program. It reads the file in question line by line and then searches for function definitions in it. The overall logic of the same can be pseudocoded as below:

```
   while not end of file
   begin
         read line
         increment count of line number
         remove whitespace at the beginning of the line
         see if the line contains a parentheses
         if not found
               continue
         search for space separated token
         if not found
               continue
         check if token is in the list of standard return types
         if not found
               continue

         check whether the line read is an assignment statement
         if an assignment statement
               continue
         copy the function information into an array of structures
   end
```

You can try to improve this program to handle multiple files or wildcards like "*.c".

# 41

# *Dynamic Memory Allocation*

M ost C programmers are familiar with dynamic memory allocation functions like *malloc()*, *calloc()*, *realloc()* etc. However, when it comes to allocating memory and then using it as an array of desired dimensions many programmers face difficulties. In this chapter I would try to address this simple yet tricky issue. I would to do so by answering the most commonly faced problems on this topic:

(a)    How would you dynamically allocate a 1-D array of integers?

```
#include "alloc.h"

#define MAX 10

main( )
{
    int *p, i ;
```

```
p = ( int * ) malloc ( MAX * sizeof ( int ) ) ;
for ( i = 0 ; i < MAX ; i++ )
{
    p[i] = i ;
    printf ( "\n%d", p[i] ) ;
}
}
```

(b)  How would you dynamically allocate a 2-D array of integers?

```
#include "alloc.h"

#define MAXROW 3
#define MAXCOL 4

main( )
{
    int *p, i, j ;
    p = ( int * ) malloc ( MAXROW * MAXCOL * sizeof ( int ) ) ;
    for ( i = 0 ; i < MAXROW ; i++ )
    {
        for ( j = 0 ; j < MAXCOL ; j++ )
        {
            p[ i * MAXCOL + j ] = i ;
            printf ( "%d ", p[ i * MAXCOL + j ] ) ;
        }
        printf ( "\n" ) ;
    }
}
```

(c)  How would you dynamically allocate a 2-D array of integers such that we are able to access any element using 2 subscripts, as in *arr[i][j]*?

```
#include "alloc.h"

#define MAXROW 3
```

```
#define MAXCOL 4

main( )
{
    int **p, i, j ;

    p = ( int ** ) malloc ( MAXROW * sizeof ( int * ) ) ;
    for ( i = 0 ; i < MAXROW ; i++ )
        p[i] = ( int * ) malloc ( MAXCOL * sizeof ( int ) ) ;

    for ( i = 0 ; i < MAXROW ; i++ )
    {
        for ( j = 0 ; j < MAXCOL ; j++ )
        {
            p[i][j] = i ;
            printf ( "%d ", p[i][j] ) ;
        }
        printf ( "\n" ) ;
    }
}
```

(d)  How would you dynamically allocate a 2-D array of integers such that we are able to access any element using 2 subscripts, as in *arr[i][j]*? Also the rows of the array should be stored in adjacent memory locations.

```
#include "alloc.h"

#define MAXROW 3
#define MAXCOL 4

main( )
{
    int **p, i, j ;

    p = ( int ** ) malloc ( MAXROW * sizeof ( int * ) ) ;
    p[0] = ( int * ) malloc ( MAXROW * MAXCOL * sizeof ( int ) ) ;
```

```
        for ( i = 0 ; i < MAXROW ; i++ )
            p[i] = p[0] + i * MAXCOL ;

        for ( i = 0 ; i < MAXROW ; i++ )
        {
            for ( j = 0 ; j < MAXCOL ; j++ )
            {
                p[i][j] = i ;
                printf ( "%d ", p[i][j] ) ;
            }
            printf ( "\n" ) ;
        }
    }
```

(e)  How would you dynamically allocate memory for a 3-D array
     and how would you free the memory that has been allocated.

     Let us first concentrate on allocating memory for a 3-D array.

```
#include "alloc.h"

#define MAXX 3
#define MAXY 4
#define MAXZ 5

main( )
{
    int ***p, i, j, k ;

    p = ( int *** ) malloc ( MAXX * sizeof ( int ** ) ) ;
    for ( i = 0 ; i < MAXX ; i++ )
    {
        p[i] = ( int ** ) malloc ( MAXY * sizeof ( int * ) ) ;
        for ( j = 0 ; j < MAXY ; j++ )
            p[i][j] = ( int * ) malloc ( MAXZ * sizeof ( int ) ) ;
    }
```

```
        for ( k = 0 ; k < MAXZ ; k++ )
        {
            for ( i = 0 ; i < MAXX ; i++ )
            {
                for ( j = 0 ; j < MAXY ; j++ )
                {
                    p[i][j][k] = i + j + k ;
                    printf ( "%d ", p[i][j][k] ) ;
                }
                printf ( "\n" ) ;
            }
            printf ( "\n\n" ) ;
        }
    }
```

(f)   Can you figure out how many bytes are allocated by the following sets of statements:

(1)   #include "alloc.h"

```
      #define MAXROW 3
      #define MAXCOL 4

      main( )
      {
          int ( *p )[MAXCOL] ;
          p = ( int ( * ) [MAXCOL] ) malloc ( MAXROW * sizeof ( *p ) ) ;
      }
```

(2)   #include "alloc.h"

```
      #define MAXROW 3
      #define MAXCOL 4

      main( )
      {
```

```
        int ( *p )[MAXCOL][MAXROW] ;
        p = ( int ( * ) [MAXROW][MAXCOL] ) malloc ( sizeof ( *p ) ) ;
}
```

(g)   Each of the above set allocates 14 bytes in memory.

To deallocate the memory allocated using the *malloc( )* family
of functions we have to use the function *free( )*. Can you write
the code to free the memory allocated by the following program?

```
#include "alloc.h"

#define MAXROW 3
#define MAXCOL 4

main( )
{
    int **p, i ;

    p = ( int ** ) malloc ( MAXROW * sizeof ( int * ) ) ;
    for ( i = 0 ; i < MAXROW ; i++ )
        p[i] = ( int * ) malloc ( MAXCOL * sizeof ( int ) ) ;
}
```

Here it is...

```
for ( i = 0 ; i < MAXROW ; i++ )
    free ( p[i] ) ;

free ( p ) ;
```

And this one I would leave for you. Write the code to free the memory
allocated by the following program?

```
#include "alloc.h"
```

```
#define MAXROW 3
#define MAXCOL 4

main( )
{
    int **p, i, j ;

    p = ( int ** ) malloc ( MAXROW * sizeof ( int * ) ) ;
    p[0] = ( int * ) malloc ( MAXROW * MAXCOL * sizeof ( int ) ) ;

    for ( i = 0 ; i < MAXROW ; i++ )
        p[i] = p[0] + i * MAXCOL ;
}
```

# 42 *Testing Programs*

Testing is part and parcel of creating a working system. However, it is one of the most neglect areas. Often testing is done only superficially, almost as an after-thought. This so happens because program developers usually want to demonstrate that their system works, not find bugs. The bugs in the system will not cease to exist because they have not been found during testing. Sooner or later they will affect the user. A well planned project should have testing as an integral part of it and should receive proper attention.

In this chapter I would first elaborate the tests that one should carry out on one's software and then show you how this can be done practically.

Any software should be subjected to the following tests during the testing phase:

(a)     Individual function testing:

        Try to test one function at a time by supplying test arguments. When individual testing is not possible test functions in as small a group of functions as possible. This way you can detect errors that would not be detected in a system-wide test. A system-wide test can check only a limited subset of all the possible combinations. Even if the system seems to work, errors in infrequently used paths might remain. These errors might then appear under unusual circumstances, and might be very difficult to detect. Individual function testing makes your code more robust.

(b)    Use test plans

A test plan is nothing but a list of things to test, clear instructions on how to perform every test, and specifications of what is success and what is failure. Test plans help you ensure that the same things will be tested in the same way, in short consistency in checking. In every part of the test plan one should specify what input should be provided, what constitutes right behavior, and what constitutes wrong behavior. A properly laid out test plan allows you to accomplish these objective.

A test plan ensures a proper transfer of information from the tester to the developer since now the developer knows what was exactly tested, and how.

(c)    Automate testing

Whenever we are to test functions we can write separate test programs. This test program should call the function with several different sets of parameters and verify the result. After you make several modifications to a library of functions, run the tests for the entire library to make sure that everything is working correctly.

This would automate testing and make it is fast, less time consuming and consistent. In test programs, one should use *assert()* to catch errors and print a message on successful completion. We can also think of modifying the functions that obtain keyboard input to read data from a file. In that file, we should provide keystrokes as if a user has typed them. If possible we can use a keyboard emulator to generate keystrokes for us. This is especially useful while testing programs that need lot of interaction with the user.

(d)     Test for special cases and extreme values

Often programs and functions fail on extreme values and on special cases than on normal values. If a program or function works correctly for a few random values well within its domain, it will probably work correctly for most others too. Once the basic algorithm is correct, most of the problems are found at the boundaries and at special values. To test boundaries, one should provide pairs of values, one right inside the range and domain, the other outside the range or domain. Also one needs to test the function/program for some special values.

(e)     Let somebody else test your program

Though difficult to digest, a person who has written the code may not be the best person to test it. The developer tends to test the cases that he or she provided for, missing potential errors or non-conformance to functional specifications. As against this, a person who did not participate in the creation of the system will not be prejudiced towards testing only the areas that are considered important by the developer or the areas that are known to be implemented. Instead, he or she might discover missing features that the developer did not consider important enough or forgot about. Also there is every likelihood that the new person might test the implemented functionality in a different way, discovering additional bugs.

Let us now see how some of the tests discussed above can be done practically.

The following test program would test the working of the function *strchr()*.

```c
#include "assert.h"

int main( )
{
    char str[ ] = "sampdoria" ;
    assert ( strchr ( str, 'k') == 0 ) ;
    assert ( strchr ( str, 'a') == str + 1 ) ;
    assert ( strchr ( str, 'a' ) + 1 == strchr ( str, 'm' ) ) ;
    assert ( strchr ( str, 'o' ) == str + 5 ) ;
    assert ( strchr ( str, '\0' ) == str + strlen ( str ) ) ;
    printf ( "\nstrchr( ) tested OK." ) ;
}
```

This program tests the function *strchr()* for correctness. Here we have used *assert()* to catch errors and print a message on successful completion. The first *assert()* tests a case where *strchr()* should return NULL. The next three statements test cases where the character should be found. The last *assert()* verifies that *strchr()* returns a pointer to the end of the search string when a null character is supplied. Since we have automated the testing of *strchr()* we can save time and achieve higher consistency. In general, while testing a function, we should create a program to call the function with several different sets of parameters and verify the result.

Let us test one more function, *pow()*. Our program should test *pow()* for special cases and extreme values.

```c
#include <assert.h>
#include <math.h>
#include <stdio.h>

int main( )
{
    double x, y ;
```

```
            errno = 0 ;
            pow ( -1, 2.5 ) ;
            assert ( errno == EDOM ) ;

            errno = 0 ;
            assert ( pow ( 2.35, 0.0 ) == 1.0 ) ;
            assert ( errno == 0 ) ;

            x = pow ( 1.0e-30, 2.5 ) ;
            assert ( errno == 0 ) ;
            printf ( "%lf", x ) ;

            x = pow ( 1.0e30, 200.5 ) ;
            assert ( errno == 0 ) ;
            printf ( "\n%lf", x ) ;

            printf ( "\nsqrt( ) tested OK." ) ;
    }
```

Most programs and functions produce valid results for input that
conforms to certain constraints. Input violating some of these constraints will generate invalid results. If the transformation that the
program or function is modeling is not defined for a given input, a
domain error occurs, On the other hand, if the transformation is
defined, but the result cannot be represented by the program or
function, a range error occurs. For example, when a negative number
is raised to a real power a domain error occurs, whereas if we raise a
number to a huge power the range error may occur.

If a program or function works correctly for a few random values well
within its domain, it will probably work correctly for most others too.
Once the basic algorithm is correct, most of the problems are found
at the boundaries and at special values. To test boundaries, we must
provide pairs of values, one right inside the range and domain, the
other outside the range or domain. Also, we should test the function
for some special values. At the very least, we should test the function

for a big and a small negative number, a big and a small positive number, zero, and one.

# 43  *The Duff's Device*

I am sure you would find the following code intriguing, since this is not the normal way in which one programs. However, interestingly the code works without any problem. Here the function copies count integers from one area of memory to another. Note that after the *switch* statement jumps into the middle of the *do-while* loop, the *case* statements are completely ignored while the loop executes.

```
void send ( register* to, register* from, register count )
{
    register n = ( count + 7 ) / 8 ;

    switch ( count % 8 )
    {
        case 0:
            do
            {
                *to++ = *from++ ;
            case 7:
                *to++ = *from++ ;
```

```
        case 6:
            *to++ = *from++ ;

        case 5:
            *to++ = *from++ ;

        case 4:
            *to++ = *from++ ;

        case 3:
            *to++ = *from++ ;

        case 2:
            *to++ = *from++ ;

        case 1:
            *to++ = *from++ ;

        } while ( --n > 0 ) ;
    }
}
```

When Tom Duff first published this code in 1984, he stated:

*Consider the following routine, abstracted from code which copies an array of shorts into the Programmed IO data register of an Evans & Sutherland Picture System II:*

```
send ( to, from, count )
register short *to, *from;
register count ;
{
    do
        *to++ = *from++ ;
    while ( --count > 0 ) ;
}
```

(Obviously, this fails if the count is zero.) The VAX C compiler compiles the loop into 2 instructions (a movw and a sobleq, I think.) As it turns out, this loop was the bottleneck in a real- time animation playback program which ran too slowly by about 50%. The standard way to get more speed out of something like this is to unwind the loop a few times, decreasing the number of sobeqs. When you do that, you wind up with a leftover partial loop. I usually handle this in C with, a switch that indexes a list of copies of the original loop body. Of course, if I were writing assembly language code, I'd just jump into the middle of the unwound loop to deal with the leftovers. Thanking about this one day last October, the following implementation occurred to me:

(above code).

Disgusting, no? But it compiles and runs just fine on all known C compilers. Dennis Ritchie has endorsed it as legal C. I feel a combination of pride and revulsion at this discovery; I think I'll name it after myself - "Duff's Device" has a nice ring to it.

The above passage has been adapted from *net.lang.c* on Internet.

Why would anyone write code like that? Any advantage in terms of speed from such programming as above is dependent on the machine and the optimizer. Hence one is better advised to do such programming only when the timing results indicate that it is necessary. Also, most of the standard C compilers provide a standard library function called *memcpy()* whose purpose is to copy blocks of memory.

# 44 *Stripping Comments*

Often to fit a program or a series of programs on a disk we try to eliminate comments present in them to reduce their sizes which maintaining their functionality intact. Here is a program for removing comments out of a C/C++ program. Both, // and /* */ type of comments are removed by it. The program assumes that the programs on which it works are grammatically correct and does not bother about the layout of the output. Here is the program...

```
#include <stdio.h>

FILE *fs, *ft ;

int main ( int argc, char*argv[ ] )
{
    char ch ;

    if ( argc != 3 )
    {
        printf ( "Correct usage: remove <source> <target>" ) ;
        exit ( 1 ) ;
```

```
        }

        fs = fopen ( argv[1], "r" ) ;
        if ( fs == NULL )
        {
            printf ( "\nUnable to open source file" ) ;
            exit ( 2 ) ;
        }

        ft = fopen ( argv[2], "w" ) ;
        if ( ft == NULL )
        {
            printf ( "\nUnable to open source file" ) ;
            fclose ( fs ) ;
            exit ( 3 ) ;
        }

        while ( ( ch = getc ( fs ) ) != EOF )
        {
            /* a / may be followed by another / or a * */
            if ( ch == '/' )
            {
                ch = getc ( fs ) ;
                if ( ch == EOF )
                    break ;

                if ( ch == '/' )
                    striplinecomment( ) ;
                else if ( ch == '*' )
                    stripblockcomment( ) ;

                /* if not one of the above, then it's
                   not a comment and the 2nd character
                   must be rescanned */
                else
                {
                    putc ( '/', ft ) ;
```

```
                ungetc ( ch, fs ) ;
            }
        }
        else   /* a printable character */
        {
            putc ( ch, ft ) ;
            if ( ch == '"' || ch == '\'' )
                stringorchar ( ch ) ;
        }
    }
}

striplinecomment( )
{
    char ch ;
    /* loop until end of line */
    while ( ( ch = getc ( fs ) ) != EOF )
    {
        if ( ch == '\n')
        {
            putc ( ch, ft ) ;
            return ;
        }
    }
    printf ( "\nstriplinecomment: EOF found within line comment" ) ;
}


stripblockcomment( )
{
    char ch ;
    putc ( ' ', ft ) ;

    /* loop until matching */
    while ( ( ch = getc ( fs ) ) != EOF )
    {
        if ( ch == '*' )
        {
```

```
                    ch = getc ( fs ) ;
                    if ( ch == EOF )
                        break ;
                    if ( ch == '/' )
                        return ;
                    ungetc ( ch, fs ) ;
            }
            else
                if (ch == '\n' )
                    putc ( ch, ft ) ;
    }
    printf ( "\nstripblockcomment: EOF found within full comment" ) ;
}


stringorchar ( char start )
{
    char ch ;
    while ( ( ch = getc ( fs ) ) != EOF )
    {
        /* copy chars within string */
        putc ( ch, ft ) ;

        /* found 2nd quote? */
        if ( ch == start )
            return ;

        /* found \x, skip past 1 char */
        if ( ch == '\\' )
        {
            ch = getc ( fs ) ;
            if ( ch == EOF )
                break ;

            putc ( ch, ft ) ;
        }
    }
    printf ( "\nstringorchar: EOF found within string or char constant" ) ;
```

}

To begin with we have opened the source file (which contains comments) and the target file (into which we must write all text of source file except the comments). It is expected that the filenames would be supplied as command line arguments.

The main loop simply copies all characters up to the end of the file, while looking for a slash, a single quote, or a double quote. If a slash is followed by another slash, a line comment has been encountered. In such a case the function *striplinecomment()* is called. If a slash is followed by an asterisk then a block comment has been encountered and to eliminate this the function *stripblockcomment()* is called. If neither a slash nor an asterisk follows the initial slash, then the initial slash should be output and the second character rescanned. A single and double quote begins either a character or string constant. Since the rule for character and string constants are so similar, they can be handled by the same function by passing in the character that started the constant. This is done by the function *stringorchar()*. The only errors detected are if the end of the file is found while in one of the comment or a constant (string or character).

The loop for line comments simply looks for newlines. When it finds one, it prints it out and returns.

The loop for block comments is similar except that it must find both an asterisk and a slash to finish the comment. If an asterisk is found followed by something other than a slash, the second character is put back on the input stream so that it can be rescanned for another asterisk. Since a block comment is equivalent to whitespace, the program outputs a single blank character to ensure that two tokens don't accidentally get joined together. Also, any newlines found are copied to keep the number of lines equivalent to what is in the source.

The loop for character and string constants simply continues until the matching quote character is found. If a backslash is found, the escape sequence that follows it must consist of at least one character. Since there is no need to fully parse the quoted character, the second character is simply read and output.

# *45* *Building Libraries*

In this chapter I would present a utility which creates one or more libraries from all "*.c" files in the current directory. While executing the program two and only two parameters are required. The first is used to specify the common name prefix for the series of generated libraries. The second parameter is a char string of one or more characters indicating desired memory models. Each library name is formed by suffixing the library series name with a character from the memory model list. The memory model list consists of contiguous characters without any surrounding quotes. Valid characters for the memory model list are: *t s m c l h* standing for tiny, small, medium, compact, large and huge memory models respectively. It is necessary that the utilities TCC and TLIB are in the current search path. Here is the program...

```
#include <dir.h>
#include <process.h>
#include <stdio.h>
#include <string.h>

#define MAX_LIBNAME_CHARS 7
```

```
#define MAX_CMD_SIZE    255

int main ( int argc, char *argv[ ] )
{
    char lib_name[MAX_LIBNAME_CHARS + 2] ;
    char *lib_mod ;
    char *lib_type ;

    if ( argc != 3 )
    {
        printf ( "\nOnly 2 parameters are required" ) ;
        printf ( "\n1st parm specifies base lib_name" ) ;
        printf ( "\n2nd parm is a char list of memory models:tsmclh" ) ;
        exit ( 1 ) ;
    }

    if ( strlen ( argv[1] ) > MAX_LIBNAME_CHARS )
    {
        printf ( "\nLength of base lib_name is too long" ) ;
        exit ( 2 ) ;
    }

    if ( strspn ( argv[2], "tsmclh" ) != strlen ( argv[2] ) )
    {
        printf ( "\nInvalid memory model specified in 2nd parameter" ) ;
        exit ( 3 ) ;
    }

    strcpy ( lib_name, argv[1] ) ;
    lib_mod = lib_name + strlen ( lib_name ) ;
    strcat ( lib_name, " " ) ;

    for ( lib_type = argv[2] ; *lib_type ; lib_type++ )
    {
        compile ( lib_type ) ;
        *lib_mod = *lib_type ;
        create_lib ( lib_name ) ;
```

```
        }
    }

/* compiles all ".c" files in the current directory with
   memory model specified by "lib_type" */
compile ( char *lib_type )
{
    static char *lib_type_pos = NULL ;
    #define LIB_TYPE_POS   '^'
    static char *compile_cmd  = "tcc -m^ -k- -a -c -G -O -Z -d *.c" ;

    if ( lib_type_pos == NULL )
        lib_type_pos = strchr ( compile_cmd, LIB_TYPE_POS ) ;

    *lib_type_pos = *lib_type ;
    system ( compile_cmd ) ;
}

/* adds "obj_name" to lib and then deletes the original. */
void add_obj ( char *lib_add_cmd, char *obj_name )
{
    char cmd[MAX_CMD_SIZE] ;
    sprintf ( cmd, "%s%s", lib_add_cmd, obj_name ) ;
    system ( cmd ) ;
    sprintf ( cmd, "del %s", obj_name ) ;
    system ( cmd ) ;
}

/* creates a library out of all object files in the current directory */
create_lib ( char *lib_name )
{
    char cmd[MAX_CMD_SIZE] ;
    struct ffblk dos_fcb ;

    if ( findfirst ( "*.obj", &dos_fcb, 0 ) == 0 )
    {
        sprintf ( cmd, "del %s.lib", lib_name ) ;
```

```
        system ( cmd ) ;
        sprintf ( cmd, "tlib %s /E +", lib_name ) ;
        add_obj ( cmd, dos_fcb.ff_name ) ;
        while ( findnext ( &dos_fcb ) == 0 )
            add_obj ( cmd, dos_fcb.ff_name ) ;
    }

    sprintf ( cmd, "del %s.bak", lib_name ) ;
    system ( cmd ) ;
}
```

# 46 A Simple Program

Suppose we wish to write a program which can generate all possible combinations of numbers from 1 to one less than the given number. The solution at first glance appears to be simple. For example, if the given number is 3 then the program that generates all the combinations would be as follows:

```
main( )
{
    int i, j, k ;
    int n = 3 ;

    for ( i = 1 ; i <= n ; i++ )
    {
        for ( j = 1 ; j <= n ; j++ )
        {
            for ( k = 1 ; k <= n ; k++ )
            {
                if ( i != j && j != k && k != i )
                    printf ( "\n%d %d %d", i, j, k ) ;
            }
```

```
            }
        }
    }
```

This is a fairly straight-forward program. However, if value of *n* is unknown at the time of writing the program then it is difficult to code the logic since how many loops are to be written would vary according to the value of *n*. To begin with I was (and am still) under the impression that this can be managed using the *paste* macro. However, one of the readers of my *C Column* (Jimmy Louis) suggested another solution using recursion. I am presenting below his solution.

```
static int used[10], sequence[10], total_digits, count = 1 ;

main( )
{
    clrscr( ) ;

    puts ( "Enter no. of digits" ) ;
    scanf ( "%d", &total_digits ) ;

    printf ( "\n\nvarious combination possible are-\n\n:" ) ;
    printf ( "SR. NO.\t\t\tCOMBINATIONS\n" ) ;

    combination ( 0 ) ;
}

combination ( int num )
{
    int i ;

    if ( num < total_digits )
    {
        for ( i = 0 ; i < total_digits ; i++ )
        {
            if ( !used[i] )
            {
```

```
                    sequence[num] = i + 1 ;
                    used[i] = 1 ;
                    combination ( num + 1 ) ;
                    used[i] = 0 ;
            }
        }
    }
    else
        display( ) ;

    return ;
}

display( )
{
    int i = 0 ;
    printf ( "%d            ", count++ ) ;

    for ( i = 0 ; i < total_digits ; i++ )
        printf ( "%d", sequence[i] ) ;

    printf ( "\n" ) ;
}
```

Recursive calls can all too easily result into run-time stack overflows that are not easy to diagnose. Moreover, the implementation doesn't resemble a normal *for* loop construct, which makes following the program logic more difficult and could add to the maintenance cost.

We can do the same job without using recursion. The following solution has been suggested by Harish Tanna of Mumbai most. I would like to share the same with the readers who also might find the same interesting.

```
main( )
{
    long start, end, cut, steps, now, cnt1, cnt2, cnt3 ;
```

```
int num, ok, icon1, icon2 ;

clrscr( ) ;
printf ( "Enter Number " ) ;
scanf ( "%d", &num) ;

num = num < 1 ? 1 : num > 9 ? 9 : num ;

for ( start=1, end=num, cut=10, steps=1, cnt1=2 ; cnt1 <= num ;
        cnt1++ )
{
    start = start * 10 + cnt1 ;
    end = end * 10 + num - cnt1 + 1 ;
    cut *= 10 ;
    steps *= cnt1 ;
}

for ( ok = 1, now = 0, cnt1 = start ; cnt1 <= end ; cnt1 += 9, ok = 1 )
{
    for ( cnt2 = 10 ; cnt2 <= cut / 10 && ok ; cnt2 *= 10 )
    {
        icon1 = cnt1 % cnt2 / ( cnt2 / 10 ) ;
        for ( cnt3 = cnt2 * 10 ; cnt3 <= cut && ok ; cnt3 *= 10 )
        {
            icon2 = cnt1 % cnt3 / ( cnt3 / 10 ) ;
            if ( icon1 == icon2 || icon1 < 1 || icon2 < 1 || icon1 > num
                || icon2 > num )
                ok = 0 ;
        }
    }

    if ( ok )
        printf ( "\nSeq.No. %ld of %ld is : %ld",++now, steps, cnt1 ) ;
}
}
```

The program determines the first and the last number of the steps (in case of 4, the first number becomes 1234 and the last 4321) and then within a loop does 3 tasks add, check and print. The program suffers from the drawback that it cannot tackle input beyond 9. To care of this drawback Harish has suggested one more program. Here it is...

```c
main( )
{
    long steps, fval, bstp, cnt1 ;
    int num, unit, box[2][13], cnt2, cnt3, cnt4 ;

    clrscr( ) ;
    printf ( "Enter Number " ) ;
    scanf ( "%d", &num ) ;

    num = num < 1 ? 1 : num > 12 ? 12 : num ;

    for ( steps = 1, cnt1 = 2 ; cnt1 <= num ; steps *= cnt1++ ) ;

    for ( cnt1 = 1 ; cnt1 <= steps ; cnt1++ )
    {
        for ( cnt2 = 1 ; cnt2 <= num ; cnt2++ )
            box[0][cnt2] = cnt2 ;

        for ( fval = steps, bstp = cnt1, cnt2 = 1 ; cnt2 <= num ; cnt2++ )
        {
            if ( bstp == 0 )
            {
                cnt4 = num ;
                while ( box[0][cnt4] == 0 )
                    cnt4-- ;
            }
            else
            {
                fval /= num - cnt2 + 1 ;
                unit = ( bstp + fval - 1 ) / fval ;
                bstp %= fval ;
```

```
                    for ( cnt4 = 0, cnt3 = 1 ; cnt3 <= unit ; cnt3++ )
                        while ( box[0][++cnt4] == 0 ) ;
                    }

                box[1][cnt2] = box[0][cnt4] ;
                box[0][cnt4] = 0 ;
            }

            printf ( "\nSeq.No.%ld:", cnt1 ) ;

            for ( cnt2 = 1 ; cnt2 <= num ; cnt2++ )
                printf ( " %d", box[1][cnt2] ) ;
        }
    }
```

This program computes the total number of steps. But instead of entering into the loop of the first and last combination to be generated it uses a loop of 1 to number of combinations. For example, in case of input being 5 the number of possible combinations would be factorial 5, i.e. 120. The program suffers from the limitation that it cannot generate combinations for input beyond 12 since a *long int* cannot handle the resulting combinations.

# 47 *A Data Entry Function*

In this chapter we propose to develop a data entry function with more or less same facilities as you get in FoxPro or other xBase software. We want that the function should not only provide a good method for entering data, but should also do basic validation of the data being entered. We would call this function as *getinput()*. *getinput()* accepts input from the user and returns to the calling program an integer value that represents a terminating key. The terminating key is the key that is pressed by the user signaling either that some action may need to be performed by the calling program or that the user is done entering data in the field. The calling program will determine what needs to be done based on that terminating key. If the terminating key is a "moving" terminating key such as Up Arrow, Down Arrow, Home, End, Tab, or Enter, then the calling program will probably want to move to the next or previous field. The following program shows the *getinput()* function as well as how to use it.

```
#include <stdio.h>
#include <conio.h>
#include <ctype.h>
```

```
#include <dos.h>
#include <string.h>

#define C_UP        328
#define C_DOWN      336
#define C_PGUP      329
#define C_PGDN      337
#define C_CR        13
#define C_BACK      8
#define C_LEFT      331
#define C_RIGHT     333
#define C_TAB       9
#define C_HOME      327
#define C_END       335
#define C_ESC       27
#define C_INS       338
#define C_DEL       339
#define CR_NO_CHG   -1  /* Enter key pressed - no changes */
#define UP_NO_CHG   -2  /* Up Arrow   - no changes */
#define TB_NO_CHG   -3  /* Tab Key- no changes */
#define DN_NO_CHG   -4  /* Down Arrow - no changes */
#define FNAME       0
#define AGE         1
#define YES         1
#define NO          0
#define M_INSERT    1
#define M_TYPEOVER  2

struct fields
{
    int row, col, help_row, help_col, min_len, max_len ;
    char match, help[81] ;
};

struct fields f[ ] =
{
    { 10, 37, 15, 35, 0, 30, 'A', "Enter your First name..." },
```

```
          { 11, 37, 15, 35, 0, 3, '#', "Enter your Age...   "}
};

int key ;

void main( )
{
    char xbuf[81], fname[31] ;
    int c, age, index ;

    fname[0] = '\0' ;
    clrscr( ) ;
    gotorc (10,25) ;
    printf ( "FIRST NAME:" ) ;
    gotorc (11,25) ;
    printf ( "AGE .......:" ) ;
    age = 0 ;
    index = FNAME ;

    while ( 1 )
    {
        switch ( index )
        {
            case FNAME:
                sprintf ( xbuf, "%-s", fname ) ;
                c = getinput ( xbuf, f[FNAME].match, f[FNAME].min_len,
                    f[FNAME].max_len, f[FNAME].row, f[FNAME].col,
                    f[FNAME].help, f[FNAME].help_row, f[FNAME].help_col ) ;

                switch ( c )
                {
                    case C_UP   :
                    case UP_NO_CHG:
                    case C_END   :
                        index = AGE ;  /* go to last screen field */
                        break ;
```

```
                case C_ESC :
                    exit ( 0 ) ;

                case C_CR :
                case C_DOWN:
                case C_TAB :
                    strcpy ( fname, xbuf ) ;

                case CR_NO_CHG:
                case DN_NO_CHG:
                case TB_NO_CHG:
                    index = AGE ;  /* go to next field */
                    break ;
            }

        gotorc ( 10, 37 ) ;
        printf ( "%-30.30s", fname ) ;
        break ;

    case AGE:
        sprintf ( xbuf, "%-d", age ) ;
        c = getinput ( xbuf, f[AGE].match, f[AGE].min_len,
                f[AGE].max_len, f[AGE].row, f[AGE].col,
                f[AGE].help, f[AGE].help_row, f[AGE].help_col ) ;

        switch ( c )
        {
            case C_UP    :
            case UP_NO_CHG:
                index = FNAME; /* go to previous field */
                break;

            case C_ESC :
                exit ( 0 ) ;

            case C_HOME:
            case C_CR :
```

```
                    case C_DOWN:
                    case C_TAB :
                        age = atoi ( xbuf ) ;

                    case CR_NO_CHG:
                    case DN_NO_CHG:
                    case TB_NO_CHG:
                        index = FNAME;  /* go to next screen field */
                        break ;
            }

            gotorc ( 11, 37 ) ;
            printf ( "%- 3d", age ) ;
            break ;
        }
    }
}

int getinput ( char *data, char match_ch, int min_len, int max_len, int
               row, int col, char *message, int help_row, int help_col )
{
    char buf [80] ;
    int terminate, index, i, mode, changed, edit, frst_key, more ;

    edit = frst_key = changed = NO ;
    mode = M_TYPEOVER ;

    size ( 0, 13 ) ;
    if ( strlen ( message ) )
    {
        gotorc ( help_row, help_col ) ;
        printf ( message ) ;
    }

    strcpy ( buf, data ) ;  /* make a copy of the default return value */

    /* fill remainder of default value with blanks  */
```

```
for ( index = strlen ( buf ) ; index < max_len ; ++index )
    buf [index] = ' ' ;

buf [index] = '\0' ;

gotorc ( row, col ) ;
printf ( buf ) ;  /* display default value for field */
gotorc ( row, col ) ;  /* position cursor at beginning of field  */

for ( index = 0, more = YES ; more ; )
{
    key = getch( ) ;  /* get input from user */
    if ( key == 0 )
        key = getch( ) + 256 ;

    switch( key )
    {
        case C_ESC :
            frst_key = NO ;
            terminate = key ;
            buf[index] = '\0' ;
            more = NO ;
            break ;

        case C_INS :
            frst_key = NO ;

            if ( mode == M_INSERT )
            {
                mode = M_TYPEOVER ;  /* set the mode to TYPEOVER */
                size ( 0, 13 ) ;  /* change cursor to block */
            }
            else
            {
                mode = M_INSERT ;  /* set the mode to INSERT */
                size ( 12, 13 ) ;  /* change cursor to normal */
            }
```

```
                    putchar ( buf[index] ) ;
                    gotorc ( row, ( col + index ) ) ;
                    break ;

            case C_BACK :
            case C_DEL :
                    frst_key = NO ;
                    changed = YES ;

                    if ( index >= max_len )
                        index = max_len - 1 ;

                    for ( i = index ; i < max_len ; i++ )
                    {
                        if ( buf[i+1] == '\0' )
                            buf[i] = ' ' ;
                        else
                            buf[i] = buf[i+1] ;
                    }

                    gotorc ( row, col ) ;
                    printf ( buf ) ;  /* redisplay the field */
                    gotorc ( row, (col + index ) ) ;  /* reposition the cursor */
                    putchar ( buf[index] ) ;
                    gotorc ( row, ( col + index ) ) ;

                    if ( key == C_DEL )
                        break ;

            case C_LEFT :
                    frst_key = NO ;

                    if ( index <= 0 )
                        break ;

                    if ( index >= max_len )
```

```
                    index = max_len -1 ;

            index-- ;
            gotorc ( row, ( col + index ) ) ;
            break ;

        case C_RIGHT:
            frst_key = NO ;
            edit = YES ;

            if ( index >= ( max_len - 1 ) )
                break ;

            index++ ;
            gotorc ( row, ( col + index ) ) ;
            break ;

        case C_HOME :
        case C_END :
            frst_key = NO ;

            if ( edit == YES )
            {
                if ( key == C_END )
                    index = end_of_fld ( buf, ( strlen ( buf ) ) ) ;
                else
                    index = 0 ;

                gotorc ( row, ( col + index ) ) ;
                break ;
            }

        case C_DOWN :
        case C_UP   :
        case C_PGDN :
        case C_PGUP :
        case C_CR   :
```

```
case C_TAB :
    frst_key = NO ;
    edit = NO ;          /* reset edit flag */
    mode = M_INSERT ;/* reset mode */


    if ( strlen ( data ) >= ( unsigned ) min_len &&
        index == 0 && changed == NO )
    {
        if ( key == C_CR )
            terminate = CR_NO_CHG ;

        if ( key == C_UP )
            terminate = UP_NO_CHG ;

        if ( key == C_DOWN )
            terminate = DN_NO_CHG ;

        if ( key == C_TAB )
            terminate = TB_NO_CHG ;

        if ( key != C_CR && key != C_UP && key != C_DOWN
            && key != C_TAB )
            terminate = key ;

        strcpy ( buf, data ) ;
        more = NO ;
        break ;
    }

    /* if minimum length requirement has been met, quit */
    if ( index >= min_len )
    {
        terminate = key ;
        more = NO ;
        break ;
    }
```

```
                    /* else ignore */
                    break ;

              default :
                   if ( index == max_len )
                       break ;

                   if ( key > 'z' )  /* ignore key above 'z' */
                       break ;

                   if ( match ( index, match_ch ) == YES )
                   {
                       edit = changed = YES ;

                       if ( frst_key == YES )
                       {
                            for ( i = 0 ; i < max_len ; i++ )
                                buf[i] = '' ;
                            frst_key = NO ;
                       }

                       if ( mode == M_INSERT )
                       {
                            /* insert character entered into the field */
                            for ( i = ( max_len - 1 ) ; i > index ; i-- )
                                buf[i] = buf[i-1] ;
                       }

                       buf[index] = ( char ) key ;
                       gotorc ( row, col ) ;
                       printf ( buf ) ;  /* redisplay the field */

                       /* reposition the cursor */
                       index++ ;
                       if ( index >= max_len )
                           index -- ;
```

```
                        gotorc ( row, ( col + index ) ) ;
                        putchar ( buf[index] ) ;
                        gotorc ( row, ( col + index ) ) ;
                    }
                break ;
            }
        }

        gotorc ( row, col ) ;
        printf( buf ) ;
        strcpy ( data, buf ) ;
        data[ ( end_of_fld ( data, ( strlen ( data ) ) ) + 1 )] = '\0' ;
        size ( 12, 13 ) ;  /* change cursor back to normal */
        return ( terminate ) ;
}


static int match ( int index, char match_ch )
{
    int matches = YES ;

    switch ( match_ch )
    {
        case '$' :  /* 0-9 or ,$. */
            if ( !isdigit ( key ) && !strchr ( ".,$", key ) )
                matches = NO ;
            break ;

        case '#' :  /* 0 - 9 */
            if ( !isdigit ( key ) )
                matches = NO ;
            break ;

        case 'A' :  /* A - Z */
            if ( !isalpha ( key ) && !strchr ( " ", key ) )
                matches = NO ;
            break ;
```

```
case 'D' :  /* Date: 0-9 or - or / or .*/
    if ( !isdigit ( key ) && !strchr ( ".-*/", key ) )
        matches = NO ;
    break ;

case 'I' :  /* a-z, A-Z, 0-9, or ;:.,/?*-$#( )'! or leading space */
    if ( !isalnum ( key ) &&
        !strchr ( " !@#$%^&*( )-_=+[{]}';:.,/?", key ) )
        matches = NO ;
    break ;

case 'Q' :  /* YyNn as reply to Yes/No question */
    if ( !strchr ( "YyNn", key ) )
        matches = NO ;
    key = toupper ( key ) ;
    break ;

case 'S' :  /* 0-9 or + or - */
    if ( !isdigit ( key ) && !strchr ( "+-", key ) )
        matches = NO ;
    break ;

case 'T' :  /* time: 0-9 or . or : */
    if ( !isdigit ( key ) && !strchr ( ".:", key ) )
        matches = NO ;
    break ;

default :
    matches = NO ;
    break ;
    }
    return ( matches ) ;
}

/* returns a 0 based index of the 1st non-blank character at the end of
   a string */
```

```
int end_of_fld ( char *string, int length )
{
    int  i ;

    for ( i = length - 1 ; i >= 0 ; i-- )
    {
        if ( string[i] != ' ' && string[i] != '\0' )
            return ( i ) ;
    }
    return ( 0 ) ;
}


/* changes cursor size */
size ( int start, int end )
{
    union REGS i, o ;

    i.h.ah = 1 ;
    i.h.ch = start ;
    i.h.cl = end ;
    int86 ( 16, &i, &o) ;
}

/* positions cursor */
gotorc ( int r, int c )
{
    union REGS i, o ;

    i.h.ah = 2 ;
    i.h.bh = 0 ;
    i.h.dh = r ;
    i.h.dl = c ;
    int86 ( 16, &i, &o ) ;
}
```

In this program besides the definitions of the special keys, there are
definitions for four other terminating keys which can be returned by

*getinput()* function. Since there are times when a data field requires specific validation, we want to know whether the user changed the data. If no changes occur, there is no need to do any validating. Therefore NO_CHANGE values for Up Arrow, Down Arrow, Tab, and Enter (and only these four keys) have been defined. They keys that a user is likely to press when through with entering information for a field. If you find that you use other terminating keys to end data input, you may add NO_CHANGE values for those keys as well. The *getinput()* function not only allows the user to enter in new data but gives the user the freedom to edit existing data without having to retype the entire field. The function is presented below:

From the *getinput()* function we have called functions like *match()* and *size()*. Of these *size()* just changes the size of the cursor to block or normal depending upon the starting and ending scan lines passed to it. The *match()* function is used to check the valid data.

The programmer can define a series of one-character codes that will represent sets of valid data. You can have as many sets as you like, and add them as often as is needed. This function is what I think makes *getinput()* powerful. Once the user has entered in the field's data, we can assume that the field is valid. *getinput()* will not allow any characters to be entered that are not defined as being correct for a particular match code. There may be times however when you will still have to do some validating when *getinput()* returns to the calling program. For example, while *getinput()* can make sure that the user enters all of the correct characters that make up a date, it does not validate the date.

# 48 *Data* *Compression*

Data compression is an important way to stretch disk space and speed up data transfers. This chapter describes a simple general- purpose data compression algorithm, called Byte Pair Encoding (BPE). This algorithm compresses data by finding the most frequently occurring pairs of adjacent bytes in the data and replacing all instances of the pair with a byte that was not in the original data. The algorithm repeats this process until no further compression is possible, either because there are no more frequently occurring pairs or there are no more unused bytes to represent pairs. The algorithm writes out the table of pair substitutions before the packed data. The program is presented below:

```
#include <stdio.h>

#define BLOCKSIZE   5000    /* maximum block size */
#define HASHSIZE    4096    /* size of hash table */
#define MAXCHARS    200     /* CHAR set per block */
#define THRESHOLD 3         /* minimum pair count */

unsigned char buffer[BLOCKSIZE] ; /* data block */
```

```
unsigned char leftcode[256] ;        /* pair table */
unsigned char rightcode[256] ;       /* pair table */
unsigned char left[HASHSIZE] ;       /* hash table */
unsigned char right[HASHSIZE] ;      /* hash table */
unsigned char count[HASHSIZE] ;      /* pair count */

int size ; /* Size of current block */

void main ( int argc, char *argv[ ] )
{
    FILE *fs, *ft ;

    if ( argc != 3 )
    {
        puts ( "Usage: compress source target\n" ) ;
        exit ( 1 ) ;
    }

    if ( ( fs = fopen ( argv[1], "rb" ) ) == NULL )
    {
        puts ( "Error opening input file" ) ;
        exit ( 2 ) ;
    }

    if ( ( ft = fopen ( argv[2], "wb" ) ) == NULL )
    {
        puts ( "Error opening output file" ) ;
        exit ( 3 ) ;
    }

    compress ( fs, ft ) ;

    fclose ( ft ) ;
    fclose ( fs ) ;
}

compress ( FILE *fs, FILE *ft )
```

```
{
    int leftch, rightch, code, oldsize ;
    int index, r, w, best, done = 0 ;

    /* compress each data block until end of file */
    while ( !done )
    {
        done = fileread ( fs ) ;
        code = 256 ;

        /* compress this block */
        for ( ; ; )
        {
            /* get next unused char for pair code */
            for ( code-- ; code >= 0 ; code-- )
                if ( code == leftcode[code] && !rightcode[code] )
                    break ;

            /* must quit if no unused chars left */
            if ( code < 0 )
                break ;

            /* find most frequently pair of chars */
            for ( best = 2, index = 0 ; index < HASHSIZE ; index++ )
                if ( count[index] > best )
                {
                    best = count[index] ;
                    leftch = left[index] ;
                    rightch = right[index] ;
                }

            /* done if no more compression possible */
            if ( best < THRESHOLD )
                break ;

            /* replace pairs in data, adjust pair counts */
            oldsize = size - 1 ;
```

```
for ( w = 0, r = 0 ; r < oldsize ; r++ )
{
    if ( buffer[r] == leftch && buffer[r+1] == rightch )
    {
        if ( r > 0 )
        {
            index = lookup ( buffer[w-1], leftch ) ;

            if ( count[index] > 1 )
                --count[index] ;
            index = lookup ( buffer[w-1], code )  ;

            if ( count[index] < 255 )
                ++count[index] ;
        }

        if ( r < oldsize-1 )
        {
            index = lookup ( rightch, buffer[r+2] ) ;

            if ( count[index] > 1 )
                --count[index] ;

            index = lookup ( code, buffer[r+2] ) ;

            if ( count[index] < 255 )
                ++count[index] ;
        }
        buffer[w++] = code ;
        r++ ; size-- ;
    }
    else
        buffer[w++] = buffer[r] ;
}

/* add to pair substitution table */
```

```
                leftcode[code] = leftch ;
                rightcode[code] = rightch ;

                /* delete pair from hash table */
                index = lookup ( leftch, rightch ) ;
                count[index] = 1 ;
            }

        filewrite ( ft ) ;
    }
}

/* reads next block from input file into buffer */
int fileread ( FILE *input )
{
    int c, index, used = 0 ;

    /* reset hash table and pair table */
    for ( c = 0 ; c < HASHSIZE ; c++ )
        count[c] = 0 ;

    for ( c = 0 ; c < 256 ; c++ )
    {
        leftcode[c] = c ;
        rightcode[c] = 0 ;
    }

    size = 0 ;

    /* read data until full or few unused chars */
    while ( size < BLOCKSIZE && used < MAXCHARS &&
            ( c = getc ( input ) ) != EOF )
    {
        if ( size > 0 )
        {
            index = lookup ( buffer[size-1], c ) ;
            if ( count[index] < 255 )
```

```
                    ++count[index] ;
            }
        buffer[size++] = c ;

        /* use rightcode to flag data chars found */
        if ( !rightcode[c] )
        {
            rightcode[c] = 1 ;
            used++ ;
        }
    }
    return c == EOF ;
}


/* returns index of character pair in hash table */
/* detected nodes have count of 1 for hashing */
int lookup ( unsigned char a, unsigned char b )
{
    int index;

    /* compute hash key from both characters */
    index = ( a ^ ( b << 5 ) ) & ( HASHSIZE - 1 ) ;

    /* search for pair or first empty slot */
    while ( ( left[index] != a || right[index] != b )
        && count[index] != 0 )

    index = ( index + 1 ) & ( HASHSIZE - 1 ) ;

    /* store pair in table */
    left[index] = a ;
    right[index] = b ;

    return index ;
}

/* writes each pair table and data block to output */
```

```
filewrite ( FILE *output )
{
    int i, len, c = 0 ;

    /* for each character 0..255 */
    while ( c < 256 )
    {
        /* if not a pair code, count run of literals */
        if ( c == leftcode[c] )
        {
            len = 1 ;
            c++ ;

            while ( len < 127 && c < 256 && c == leftcode[c] )
            {
                len++ ;
                c++ ;
            }

            putc ( len + 127, output ) ;

            len = 0 ;
            if ( c == 256 )
                break ;
        }

        /* else count run of pair codes */
        else
        {
            len = 0 ;
            c++ ;

            while ( len < 127 && c < 256 && c != leftcode[c] ||
                    len < 125 && c < 254 && c+1 != leftcode[c+1] )
            {
                len++ ;
                c++ ;
```

```
                    }

                    putc ( len , output ) ;
                    c -= len + 1 ;
          }

          /* write range of pairs to output */
          for ( i = 0 ; i <= len ; i++ )
          {
                    putc ( leftcode[c], output ) ;

                    if ( c != leftcode[c] )
                            putc ( rightcode[c], output ) ;

                    c++ ;
          }
     }

     /* write size bytes and compressed data block */
     putc ( size / 256, output ) ;
     putc ( size % 256, output ) ;
     fwrite ( buffer, size, 1, output ) ;
}
```

Our data compression algorithm spends most of its time in finding the most frequent pair of adjacent characters in the data. The program maintains a hash table consisting of arrays *left[ ]*, *right[ ]* and *count[ ]* to count pair frequencies. The hash table size *HASHSIZE* must be a power of two, and should not be to much smaller than the buffer size *BLOCKSIZE* or an overflow may occur. The parameter *THRESHOLD*, which specifies the minimum occurrence count of pairs to be compressed, can also be adjusted.

Once the algorithm finds the most frequently occurring pair, it must replace the pair throughout the data buffer with an unused character. The algorithm performs this replacement in place within a single buffer. As it replaces each pair, the algorithm updates the hash table's pair counts.

Having seen the BPE compression algorithm let us now have a look at the expansion algorithm. The expansion algorithm operates in a single pass. It obtains input bytes from one of the two sources, the input file, or a stack. Irrespective of an input byte's source, the algorithm processes each byte according to the following rule: If the byte is a literal, the algorithm passes it to the output; if the byte represents a pair, the algorithm replaces it with a pair and pushes the pair on to the stack.

The algorithm selects its input source according to the following rule: If the stack contains data, the algorithm obtains its next input byte from the stack. If the stack is empty, the algorithm obtains its next input byte from the input file. The following program implements this expansion algorithm.

```
#include<stdio.h>

void main ( int argc, char *argv[ ] )
{
    FILE *fs, *ft;

    if ( argc != 3 )
    {
        puts ( "Usage: expand infile outfile\n" ) ;
        exit ( 1 ) ;
    }

    if ( ( fs = fopen ( argv[1], "rb" ) ) == NULL )
    {
        puts ( "Error opening input file" ) ;
        exit ( 2 ) ;
    }

    if ( ( ft = fopen ( argv[2], "wb" ) ) == NULL )
```

```
    {
        puts ( "Error opening output file" ) ;
        exit ( 3 ) ;
    }

    decompress ( fs, ft ) ;

    fclose ( ft ) ;
    fclose ( fs ) ;
}

decompress ( FILE *input, FILE *output )
{
    unsigned char left[256], right[256], stack[30] ;
    short int c, count, i, size ;

    /* unpack each block until end of file */
    while ( ( count = getc ( input ) ) != EOF )
    {
        /* set left to itself as literal flag */
        for ( i = 0 ; i < 256 ; i++ )
            left[i] = i ;

        /* read pair table   */
        for ( c = 0 ; ; )
        {
            /* skip range of literal bytes*/
            if ( count > 127 )
            {
                c += count - 127 ;
                count = 0 ;
            }
            if ( c == 256 )
                break;

            /* read pairs, skip right if literals*/
            for ( i = 0 ; i <= count ; i++, c++ )
```

```
        {
            left[c] = getc ( input ) ;

            if ( c != left[c] )
                    right[c] = getc ( input ) ;
        }

    if ( c == 256 )
        break;

    count = getc ( input ) ;
}

/* calculate packed data block size*/
size = 256 * getc ( input ) + getc ( input ) ;

/* unpack data block */
for ( i = 0 ; ; )
{
    /* pop byte from stack or read byte*/
    if ( i )
        c = stack[--i] ;
    else
    {
        if ( !size-- )
            break;
        c = getc ( input ) ;
    }

    /* output byte or push pair on stack */
    if ( c == left[c] )
        putc ( c, output ) ;
    else
    {
        stack[i++] = right[c] ;
        stack[i++] = left[c] ;
    }
```

```
            }
        }
    }
```

# 49 *A Simple Optimization Tip*

Once the program starts running one starts looking for ways to speed up the code. At such times it is useful to pay attention to the nesting order in your loops. Simply reordering the array indexes in nested loops can offer a surprising gain in speed. For example, the program given below performs the same operation twice - in slightly different ways, but at different speeds.

```
#include "stdio.h"
#include "stdlib.h"
#include "time.h"
#include "math.h"

#define MAX 100

main( )
{
    clock_t begin, diff1, diff2 ;
```

```
int i, j ;
int arr1[MAX][MAX], arr2[MAX][MAX] ;

begin = clock( ) ;
for ( i = 0 ; i < MAX ; i++ )
{
    for ( j = 0 ; j < MAX ; j++ )
        arr1[i][j] = i + j ;
}
diff1 = clock( ) - begin ;

begin = clock( ) ;
for ( i = 0 ; i < MAX ; i++ )
{
    for ( j = 0 ; j < MAX ; j++ )
        arr2[j][i] = i + j ;
}
diff2 = clock( ) - begin ;

printf ( "\n\n%5.2f %5.2f", diff1 / ( double ) CLOCKS_PER_SEC,
                diff2 / ( double ) CLOCKS_PER_SEC ) ;
}
```

In the first set of *for* loops the outer loop manages the first array index whereas the inner loop manages the second index. In the second case it's done the other way round. On my machine, case 1 (outer loop iterates first index) executed in 0.56 seconds whereas case 2 (outer loop iterates second index) executed in 0.87 seconds.

To understand why this so happened you may recall that computer memory is logically arranged as a single large address space. One-dimensional arrays are formed by placing identical-size elements one after another in this space. In C and C++ multidimensional arrays are merely arrays of one-dimensional arrays. Thus the statement

```
int arr[3][3] = {
                    { 11, 23, 1 },
                    { 13, 14, 2 },
                    { 2, 15, 18 }
            };
```

declares an array which consists of 3 one-dimensional arrays each of three integers. So the rows and columns are only our imagination; in memory all the integers are stored linearly.

In our program the first set of loops would visit such an array's memory in the order 11-23-1-13-14-2-2-15-18. As against this, the next set of loops would visit memory in the order 11-13-2-23-14-15-1-2-18. This second sequence results into jumping around in memory. Jumping around doesn't hurt performance when arrays are small, but when arrays are large, each jump may cause an expensive cache miss or page fault. The actual performance difference depends a lot upon platform, varying not only with platform type, but also with amount of memory and cache installed and with various operating system settings.

Remember that the index order in C and C++ is row-wise, whereas in Pascal and FORTRAN the order is columnwise. So, depending on how arrays are implemented in those languages, you may have to use the opposite ordering rule while programming in those languages.

# 50 *Another Optimization Tip*

W hile writing mathematical expressions/formulae in programs we often write them just as they appear in textbooks. However, one should give careful thought before coding these formulae into valid expressions. If we modify these expressions suitably there can be sufficient gains in efficiency. For example, the square root function, *sqrt()* is time consuming and one should try to eliminate it from the formulae/expression, if possible. Suppose we have an array of coordinates of points and we wish to find the point from this array which is nearest to a given point. The distance between any point and the given point can be calculated as follows:

```
dist = sqrt ( dx * dx + dy * dy ) ;
```

where *dx* is the difference in x-coordinates and *dy* is the difference in y-coordinates. This way we can find the distance between each point in the array and the given point and then proceed to find the shortest distance. The program which achieves this in two different ways is shown below:

```c
#include "stdio.h"
#include "stdlib.h"
#include "time.h"
#include "math.h"

#define MAX 16000

main( )
{
    clock_t begin, end, diff1, diff2 ;
    int i, j, dx, dy, ptx = 5, pty = 5 ;
    double min, dist ;
    int arr[MAX][2] ;

    randomize( ) ;
    for ( i = 0 ; i < MAX ; i++ )
    {
        arr[i][0] = random ( 10 ) ;
        arr[i][1] = random ( 10 ) ;
        printf ( "\n%d %d" , arr[i][0], arr[i][1] ) ;
    }

    begin = clock( ) ;
    dx = arr[0][0] - ptx ;
    dy = arr[0][1] - pty ;
    min = sqrt ( dx * dx + dy * dy ) ;

    for ( i = 1 ; i < MAX ; i++ )
    {
        dx = arr[i][0] - ptx ;
        dy = arr[i][1] - pty ;
        dist = sqrt ( ( double ) dx * dx + dy * dy ) ;
        if ( dist < min )
            min = dist ;
```

```
          }

          end = clock( ) ;
          diff1 = end - begin ;

          begin = clock( ) ;
          dx = arr[0][0] - ptx ;
          dy = arr[0][1] - pty ;
          min = dx * dx + dy * dy ;

          for ( i = 1 ; i < MAX ; i++ )
          {
              dx = arr[i][0] - ptx ;
              dy = arr[i][1] - pty ;
              dist = dx * dx + dy * dy ;
              if ( dist < min )
                  min = dist ;
          }

          end = clock( ) ;
          diff2 = end - begin ;
          printf ( "\n\n%5.2f %5.2f", diff1 / ( double ) CLOCKS_PER_SEC,
                      diff2 / ( double ) CLOCKS_PER_SEC ) ;

      }
```

On my machine, the first method took 1.9 seconds whereas the second (no square root) took 1.0 seconds - a speed-up of nearly a factor of 2. Here we had to make *dist* and *min* as *double*s because *sqrt()* works on *double*s. In many applications the coordinates will be integers, so eliminating the *sqrt()* will eliminate all use of floating-point for an even greater speed gain.

If the formula contains an expression 'distance squared' then don't make the mistake of calculating distance first and then squaring it!

# 51  *Nested for Statements*

In Chapter 46 we had seen programs which could generate unique combinations of numbers from 1 to the any given number. I had shown how to manage this using recursion and arrays. Since then I twice encountered the situation where the number of looping variables and hence the corresponding nested *for* statements were indeterminate. Thus, only at run time could I know the nesting depth. Hence I decided to generalise the situation and came up with the program given below.

```
#include "stdio.h"

#define MAX 10

main( )
{
    int arr[MAX], begin[MAX], end[MAX], lastsub ;
    int n, i ;
    printf ( "Enter any number" ) ;
    scanf ( "%d", &n ) ;
```

```
lastsub = n - 1 ;
for ( i = 0 ; i <= lastsub ; i++ )
{
    begin[i] = 1 ;
    end[i]  = n ;
}

clrscr( ) ;

/*  explicitly nested for statements. The number of for's
    would change depending upon the value of n */
for ( arr[0] = begin[0] ; arr[0] <= end [0] ; arr[0]++ )
{
    for ( arr[1] = begin[1] ; arr[1] <= end[1] ; arr[1]++ )
    {
        for ( arr[2] = begin[2] ; arr[2] <= end [2] ; arr[2]++ )
            work ( arr, lastsub ) ;
    }
}

getch( ) ;
printf ( "\n\n" ) ;

/* recursively nested for statements */
recfor ( arr, begin, end, 0, lastsub ) ;
}

recfor ( int *arr, int *bval, int *eval, int p, int lastsub )
{
    arr[p] = bval[p] ;
    while ( arr[p] <= eval[p] )
    {
        if ( p == lastsub )
            work ( arr, lastsub ) ;
        else
            recfor ( arr, bval, eval, ( p + 1 ), lastsub ) ;
```

```
                arr[p]++ ;
        }
    }

work ( int *arr, int lastsub )
{
    int p, j, num ;

    for ( p = 0 ; p <= lastsub ; p++ )
    {
        num = arr[p] ;
        for ( j = p + 1 ; j <= lastsub ; j++ )
        {
            if ( num == arr[j] )
                return ;
        }
    }

    for ( p = 0 ; p <= lastsub ; p++ )
        printf ( "arr[%d] = %d ", p, arr[p] ) ;

    printf ( "\n" ) ;
    getch( ) ;
}
```

In the above program you will be required to only change the function *work()* to suit your specific problem. Before I wrote this program I toyed with a couple of inelegant solutions. I coded the largest number of nested *for* loops likely to be used, and then tested in each *for* whether the next *for* should be executed or not. Another alternative solution was to allow each such "extra" for statement to be executed one time but then filter out the unwanted looping variables in the body of the innermost *for* where the main calculation work is to be done. I found these solutions complex and moreover are very specific to the application at hand.

The above program implements the *for* statement as a recursive function, *recfor( )*, so that the degree of nesting may be determined at run time. The looping variables are kept in the array *arr[ ]*, where the variable *arr[loop]* iterates over integral values from *begin[p]* to *end[p]*.

No doubt the program would become slow when we use recursion in place of iteration. But at the same time it permits clean coding of a nested constructs when the depth of nesting is known only at run time.

# *Index*

# READER'S EVALUATION

I t is our sincere endeavour to publish books which are specifically designed to meet your requirements. Your feedback on our titles would be of crucial help to us in this endeavour. Please spare some of your valuable time to fill the form given below and mail it to:

*Publishing Manager,*

## BPB Publications,

20, Ansari Road, Daryaganj, New Delhi 110002

Looking forward to receiving your valuable comments and suggestions.

**Title:** **C PEARLS**

**Author:** Y. P. Kanetkar                    **ISBN:** 81-7029-859-8

Please tick the appropriate box below each question as per the following rating code:

1. COVERAGE (have all relevant topics been included in the book?)

| Excellent | Good | Average | Bad |
|-----------|------|---------|-----|

2. PRESENTATION (have the topics been clearly explained?)

| Excellent | Good | Average | Bad |
|-----------|------|---------|-----|

3. DEPTH (have the topics been explained in sufficient detail.?)

| Excellent | Good | Average | Bad |
|-----------|------|---------|-----|

4. EXAMPLES/SAMPLE PROGRAMS/EXERCISES (Are these clear and illustrative?)

| Excellent | Good | Average | Bad |
|-----------|------|---------|-----|

5. Is there any other topic which you would like to be included in the book?
   (i)
   (ii)
   (iii)

6. Is there any topic which you feel should be explained in a better manner?
   (i)
   (ii)
   (iii)

7. Is there any other book on this subject which you have been using? If yes, please state title, author and publisher.

8. How does this book compare with the other one?
   (i)    Coverage in this book is better/much better/same/worse.
   (ii)   Presentation in this book is better/much better/same/worse.
   (iii)  Depth in this book is more/much more/same/lesser.
   (iv)   Examples/sample programs in this book are better/much better/ same/worse.

9. Did you experience any difficulty in obtaining this book in your town? Yes/No

10. How did you come to know about this book?
   (i)    From friends/fellow students
   (ii)   From teacher/instructor
   (iii)  Saw it in the bookshop
   (iv)   Through an advertisement/book reviews in magazine(s).

Name: _____

Affiliation: _____

Qualification: _____

Address: _____

_____